DUNCAN MCNAMARA

WALK THIS WAY

OIL ON WATER PRESS

OIL ON WATER PRESS
This edition first published in 2023
office@oilonwaterpress.com

WALK THIS WAY

A CIP catalogue record for this book is
available from the British Library

ISBN   978-1-915316-25-7 (paperback)
ISBN   978-1-915316-26-4 (ebook)

OIL ON WATER. ORIGINAL TRUE-LIFE STORIES & MEMOIR.

Exclusive content at OILONWATERPRESS.COM

CONTENTS

||||||||||||||||||||||||||||||||||||||||||||||||||||||

For Dad.
You were always right, even when you were wrong.

O

DEATH BECOMES HIM

||||||||||||||||||||||||||||||||||||||||||||||||||||||||||||||||||||||||||||||||||||||||||||||||||||||||||||||||||||||||||||||

WHEN MY FATHER passed away in January 2020, the unenviable task of combing extensive records to compile the assets that made up his estate fell to me. The combination of his sudden death with his propensity to keep any and all documentation pertaining to financial transactions turned what should have been a single afternoon of filing and phone calls into a week-long, frustrating slog through ring binders full of correspondence which, although neatly collated, did not have a discernible order or starting point. While it was perfectly reasonable that I did not have an intimate knowledge of my father's financial status, I was shocked to learn my mother was even more oblivious when it came to practically everything in this area. Life insurance, pensions, bank accounts (and the amounts in them) were just a few of the topics never discussed between my parents. In their 39 years of marriage, Dad had steadfastly refused to allow Mum to worry herself with even the smallest amount of administration, leaving her totally at sea now the time had come to get his affairs in order. For her sake, I could leave no stone unturned.

As I tackled a particularly insipid pile of old car insurance policy illustrations that I found nestled between a holiday booking from 2011 and a receipt for a fountain pen purchased in 1981, I happened across a computer print-out of a map of northern Spain, all over which my father's distinctive handwriting could be found. I initially turned straight past it, not wanting to lose the momentum I had spent that morning building up but soon found myself drawn back to it due to the precise depiction. To my knowledge, Dad had only ever been to Spain once (a holiday to the Costa del Sol in 1998), so why would a map of a part of Spain he had never been to be important enough to keep filed away?

Upon closer inspection, the map was that of the Camino Frances, a 500 mile long walking trail that begins in the south of France before stretching west across northern Spain to the city of Santiago, commonly known as 'The Way'. I had completed The Way in the summer of 2014, but only at that moment become aware that my father had been tracking my progress while I did so. Names of towns and villages with accompanying dates had been jotted down hastily in the margins as a way of logging all the places I had been to and when during my trip. The trip itself had barely crossed my own mind in the intervening years and certainly was never discussed between my father and me before, during or after my Camino. Since the only person I spoke to while on my trip was my wife, I could only assume Dad had been gleaning information from her, although I have no idea if this was done covertly or by straight-up asking. His reasons for doing so will never be known for sure but, since I was now a father myself, I can only assume that the feelings of worry a parent carries for their child must have weighed heavily on him, as it currently does for me. As I cast my mind back, scarcely during the entire endeavour did I ever feel unsafe, yet there was no way for him to know that. I suppose you can never shake the worry of where your children are, hoping that they are happy and safe, a lifetime of which I have to come. Amongst the sea of grief I now found myself in, it was comforting, perhaps even amusing, to imagine my dad hunched over his map, worrying about his little 348-month-old. No matter his reasons, I sat in the same office chair that he would have as he tracked my movements, finally understanding that I would have loved to have talked with him about my Camino if I had known he held even the slightest interest. I pocketed the map with the realisation that those words would remain forever unspoken, a wave of regret washing over me. I haven't shed a tear for the loss of my father since he passed, yet remain terrified that my emotions would betray me at the worst possible moment, although no sudden onset of emotion has been forthcoming, whether visiting him in the chapel of rest, pallbearing or delivering his eulogy. What was, however, was my increased reliance on alcohol, something that crept up on me quite unexpectedly. My understandably concerned wife pointed out that not a day passed in that January or February without me having at least one drink, with most days many more joining them. That had to stop.

On the day before dad's funeral, I needed to drive to Liverpool John Lennon Airport to fit as many Irish relatives as possible into my Honda Civic. Stuck in traffic, I turned on the radio to hear a scientist being interviewed about a concerning number of cases in Wuhan, China, involving a novel coronavirus that had been given the stopgap name of COVID-19. Unconcerned at an epidemic over five and a half thousand miles away, I collected my kin before joining 200 other mourners in giving my father the send-off he deserved the next day. Little were we to know how it would be the last major gathering any of us would be having for the foreseeable future.

As January wore on, events surrounding coronavirus were gathering pace. On the 29th of January, a 23-year-old Chinese national enrolled at the University of York took ill with a fever, dry cough and muscle pain — symptoms we would all learn to be telltale signs. The UK had its first confirmed case of coronavirus. Despite this, I still felt a reassuring level of detachment from the issue. That was, until an email was sent out to my company's entire office on the evening of Sunday the 1st of March, informing all employees that someone in our company had tested positive for COVID. While they were understandably unable to divulge a name, it was disclosed that this person was confirmed to have spent at least a fortnight moving all around the premises, leaving no alternative but to close the building. Suddenly after being told for several years that doing so was an impossibility, working from home was to be mandatory. A few days later, on the 5th of March, the UK recorded its first coronavirus death, with the World Health Organisation declaring the situation a global pandemic on the 11th. On the 23rd of March, British Prime Minister Boris Johnson closed schools as part of a national lockdown.

With a stay at home order in place, a considerable adaptation to our behaviour was required. Now there was no excuse not to carry out the plethora of small jobs that had built up around the house, try as I might. While working from home now meant I was always at work, the ability to dip in and out of it throughout the day certainily made me a more productive and efficient worker. As I was rearranging my 'office', I once again found dad's Camino map, prompting me to dig out the old shoebox in the depths of the wardrobe in which I kept the various trinkets from my adventure. Buried underneath postcards, lighters and keyrings was a small, black notebook that I had used to chronicle my experience.

I opened it to see that a spider had fallen into a pot of ink and wandered across the pages, only to then realise it was actually my handwriting, which looked as if it had been written on horseback. With an abundance of time on my hands, I spent the next couple of days painstakingly deciphering my own diary in hopes of creating a permanent record of my Camino and, by the time I had typed up all there was, just over six thousand words lay before me. From there, I decided to use my exploits as a springboard from which I would tell the history of The Way itself, from genesis to portrayal in popular culture. I hope you enjoy it.

1

WAYS AND MEANS

IIIIIIIIIIIIIIIIIIIIIIIIIIIIIIIIIIIIIIIIIIIIIIIIIIIIIIIIIIIIIIIIIIIIIIIIIIIIIIIIIIIIIIIIIIIIIIIIIIIIIIII

ANYONE FAMILIAR WITH satellite TV would probably agree that the vast majority of channels are destined to be nothing more than passing scenery as you zip through them at the speed of sound when you should be going to bed. On the evening of the 9th of April 2011, I found myself in that exact situation. I was staying with my parents that weekend to help them declutter their garage and melted into the sofa to find something to stare at while I ate a depression-inducing microwave lasagna. As I hurtled through channel numbers high enough to give one a nosebleed, the battery in the remote had had enough, leaving me in a TV no man's land between evangelical preachers and disappointing erotica. While I can't remember the exact name of the station or the number, it was instantly recognisable as a travel channel and was partway through broadcasting the first episode of a documentary series following a Spanish musician, whose name completely escapes my memory, on his pilgrimage along the 500-mile route across northern Spain called the Camino de Santiago. This 'Camino' was totally unfamiliar to me but the word 'pilgrimage' seemed a tad pious for what appeared to be nothing more than a walking holiday and, owing to my career in in-flight entertainment, I was well used to such fare. Usually, I dislike this genre of television, mostly because I just can't get on board with the lack of realism. Are we supposed to ignore the fact that these people are travelling such large distances but are never seen carrying bags or struggling to communicate with native speakers, not to mention paying for anything? A therapist would (probably correctly) assert I was jealous. Suppose I could launch out into whatever far-flung part of the world that I wanted to so easily, with an army of porters and a cartoon money bag with a dollar sign on the side. In that case, I am reasonably confident that I would not be sitting before a computer screen watching someone else do it. Since neither going to bed nor searching for batteries were in my near future, he was going, and I was going with him.

The show's premise was summed up at regular intervals pretty succinctly: a man, apparently sick of having too much going for him, decides to set off walking the famous El Camino de Santiago de Compostela. The route itself has many names but is most commonly known in English as The Way of St James and was popularised most recently in the 2010 film *The Way*, starring Martin Sheen. There are several starting points to this pilgrimage, but all lead to the shrine of the apostle, St. James , in the Cathedral of Santiago de Compostela in Galicia, northwestern Spain, where the Saint's remains are said to be kept. We, the humble viewers, were going to journey with our musician along the most common route, The Camino Frances or The French Way. Audibly, I groaned when he actually used the phrase "to find myself" in a sentence.

So off he set, absurdly carrying nothing other than his guitar, as he set off from the traditional starting point of St-Jean-Pied-de-Port in the Pyrenean foothills. I was entirely surprised to see how beautiful the place was; cobbled streets leading to quaint bridges over the river, old houses with balconies from which one could overlook our trope as he embarked on his quest. Despite the cynic in me grumpily speculating that the town was, in all likelihood, cleaned up in anticipation of the crew's arrival, the sense of nothing but the open road ahead of him served only to slowly fill me with envy, maybe even resentment. Perhaps I regretted the choices that led me to watch people have adventures like these rather than seek them out myself and was simply making excuses for a situation entirely under my control. It was only walking, after all — putting one foot in front of the other. What exactly was stopping me? Having no answer, I made a mental note to do some research on this so-called Camino, but not too much — lest I get easily carried away and be booking plane tickets in time for breakfast. Twenty minutes later the episode ended with our protagonist struggling to pull a donkey that shared a name with an ex-girlfriend of mine along the trail. In my opinion, the animal's appearance was as sudden as it was unexplained, but what goes on in the privacy of his hotel room is none of my business. As I moved on to other tasks, the whole topic was pushed safely to the back of my mind before the day was even over. This wasn't the first time I had been carried away by the romance of dropping everything to go all the way and back again, so I decided to let my subconscious mull it over for the time being, during which it came to the fore several times. Less than a week later, however, everything was to change.

It was a Friday night, and I had been out for a meal with my wife and a few friends, followed by a few drinks in a nearby bar. I can remember having a fantastic time because, for once, I liked my wife's friends and was glad to see her enjoying herself. I remember leaving the bar at around 9 p.m. and heading out to find a taxi but this is the last memory I have of that evening before awakening in tremendous pain at Wythenshawe hospital the following day. Over the next few hours, it was explained to me by police, doctors and my wife that I had been subjected to a savage and unprovoked attack by a group of four men. I was partially blinded, my mouth had been relieved of several teeth, my jaw bone resembled the debris you find when you reach the end of a box of cornflakes, and my general appearance brought to mind a Picasso interpretation of my own face. However, the worst was yet to come. It was the expression on my mother's face when she first walked into the ward that had me reeling — the kind of look that shifted my thoughts from thinking, "I might phone in sick on Monday" to "Are whole head transplants a thing?" Now I felt compelled to be comfort *her*, but garbled speech was all that would pass my lips since it isn't easy to make oneself understood while the bottom jaw is trying to escape from the rest of the face. It was dawning on me that it could easily have been a morgue in which she was visiting me rather than a hospital wheelchair with a little less luck as unfortunately so-called 'one punch' killings are not abnormal. On the 31st of August 2014, in my hometown of Manchester, 49-year-old Michael Carter was punched during an altercation after a night out. Carter hit his head on the pavement when he fell and died in hospital several days later. I had taken enough punishment to kill twenty Michael Carters, yet here I was. I listened earnestly to the doctor as he explained how lucky I was, but the contrasting feeling washing over me was a curious mixture of good and bad luck during my stay. I had surgery and was discharged a week later and over the next couple of years I had several procedures to realign my jaw alongside a series of painful dental surgeries. Unfortunately, the doctors eventually managed to restore my appearance rather than improve it, and the career as a model regrettably continues to elude me.

However, I soon began a battle that I was not anticipating. Until the end of my medical procedures, I was able to focus my complete attention on my physical recovery, yet as time wore on, the attack slowly began to take its toll on my mental health, and I started withdrawing from socialising. I now hated crowds and could no longer abide going anywhere where someone would be able to approach me from behind. Eventually, in February 2012, the only two attackers arrested were to have their day in court. My wife and I were invited to Manchester crown court the week before the trial date by Victim Support, an independent charity dedicated to supporting victims of crime in England and Wales. They gave us a tour of the courts with the intention of making it less intimidating for us on the day we were to provide evidence, something that was an enormous help, particularly to my wife, who had been immensely traumatised by what had happened. Although outwardly calm, it was a curious feeling to be the victim but be less affected by the incident that made me so, owing to my total lack of memory. How was I going to feel on the day the trial started? I would be able to see the complete stranger sitting mere yards away that is (allegedly) responsible for us all being there.

On the morning of the trial, one of the defendants lost his nerve, changing his plea to guilty, eventually being ordered to pay me a victim surcharge of £500, which I used as a deposit on the £8000 needed to have my teeth repaired. Regrettably the remaining defendant dug his heels in, and the trial was expected to last three days. Fortunately, we were only expected to be there to give our evidence, after which we went home to await the verdict. It was on the fourth day that we received the call from the detective handling our case. Not guilty. The detective seemed authentic in his disquiet that the judgement was, in his words, "only a partial success". So out of the four perpetrators, only two were ever caught, and only one was convicted, a conclusion that was a very bitter pill to swallow. I learned a few years later that the young man who was found not guilty for the attack had been killed in a road traffic accident at the age of 22 — which left me with mixed emotions. I wanted him punished, but I wasn't thankful he was dead and while I am unsure if it is because he passed away, I do think about him a lot less now. The trial's outcome took its toll however, culminating with my severe anxiety and depression diagnosis in August 2012. Without the support of my family, I dread to think about where those conditions may have led me but a combination of medication and counselling followed, setting me on the road to recovery that would eventually lead to St Jean on the 10th of June 2014.

In the UK, we have an agency called the Criminal Injuries Compensation Authority (CICA), which administers a scheme that awards financial compensation to blameless victims of violent crime. On top of the depression and physical recovery, I didn't feel up for the fight of convincing someone through a written personal statement the extent to which I deserved to be compensated and decided to have a lawyer set this up for me. That way, all I had to do was wait. So I waited. And waited. And waited. Finally, in February 2014, I was presented with a figure that CICA deemed fair compensation for my injuries, a figure to which I acquiesced. CICA runs a fantastic service that has been crucial to thousands of recoveries since it launched in 1996, but something about the government paying for the violent crimes of some individuals didn't sit well with me. This wasn't fair. I now had a new level of resentment towards these thugs, this time as a citizen, although I soon took comfort in the fact that I felt equipped to move on with my life due to all the support I received. Then I remembered the Spanish musician who went for a walk and knew I had to put this all behind me — about 500 miles should do it.

2

ANY WHICH WAY

||||||||||||||||||||||||||||||||||||||||||||||||||||||||||||||||||||||||||||||||||||||

The pilgrim route is a very good thing, but it is narrow. For the road which leads us to life is narrow; on the other hand, the road which leads to death is broad and spacious. The pilgrim route is for those who are good: it is the lack of vices, the thwarting of the body, the increase of virtues, pardon for sins, sorrow for the penitent, and the road of the righteous, love of the saints, faith in the resurrection and the reward of the blessed, a separation from hell, the protection of the heavens. It takes us away from luscious foods, it makes gluttonous fatness vanish, it restrains voluptuousness, constrains the appetites of the flesh which attack the fortress of the soul, cleanses the spirit, leads us to contemplation, humbles the haughty, raises up the lowly, loves poverty. It hates the reproach of those fueled by greed. It loves, on the other hand, the person who gives to the poor. It rewards those who live simply and do good works, and, on the other hand, it does not pluck those who are stingy and wicked from the claws of sin.

—Codex Calixtinus

THE CAMINO DE Santiago goes by many names. The Way of St James, St James' Way, St James' Trail, Route of Santiago de Compostela and Road to Santiago, to name but a few, but is most commonly known simply as, The Way. While most pilgrims walk for spiritual reasons, The Way has become increasingly popular with hikers, cyclists and organised tours. During the middle ages, the route had become one of the most important Christian pilgrimages, but historical events such as the Protestant Reformation and the Black Death all but eliminated the pilgrimage as an attraction until as recently as the 1980s. The name itself is a misnomer that can easily mislead one into thinking there is only one way. In fact, there are dozens of recognised routes to Santiago originating around Europe. If one was to subscribe to the idea that the Camino truly begins at one's front door, the number of ways quickly becomes countless. Starting in southwestern France and leading to Cape Finisterre in Galicia, the main pilgrimage route can actually thank an old Roman trade route for its existence, eventually leading pilgrims to what the Romans considered the westernmost point of the world.

The Way is adorned throughout with images of the scallop shell, abundant on the shores of Galicia, and long considered the symbol of the Camino. As time has marched on like the proverbial pilgrim, the meaning of the shell has gone from the mythical to the practical, from symbolising the route to literally marking out the Way for pilgrims, even adorning the homes of pilgrims past in the form of a souvenir. The actual origin of the shell's symbolism range from utterly ridiculous to totally absurd. In the earliest version, Saint James' body was shipped back to Galicia from Judea upon his death, during which it was caught in a heavy storm, causing the body to be lost. It returned after several days at sea, however, undamaged and covered in sea scallops. In another version, James' body, still returning to Galicia for burial, was aboard a ship piloted by an angel. It was at this time that the vessel caught the sight of a groom's horse at a nearby wedding, causing it to bolt into the ocean. In this instance, it was the horse to emerge from the water covered in scallops. Much like the clover was used to explain the holy trinity to early Irish Christians, the shell can also be used as a metaphor in the same way, whereby the grooves in the shell represent the different routes of the Camino converging on the same destination, the tomb of St James, and many pilgrims believe that the shell represents God's hand guiding them, much as the sea guides the shells to the shore. At one time, the shell served a more practical purpose, being used as a makeshift drinking or eating utensil, although this use has all but disappeared. The shell can be seen countless times along the trail to guide pilgrims, including tiles on posts, painted on walls or in the form of ornate metal decorations lining the pavement — not to mention adorned by the pilgrims themselves when they collect one at the start of their journey. While one can quickly identify a pilgrim without a shell, many take pride in wearing one, officially identifying oneself as a pilgrim. The tradition of returning to home in possession of one of these shells is almost as old as the pilgrimage itself.

Records of pilgrimages originating from beyond the Pyrenees go back to the 11th century, although you have to look at the 12th century to see evidence of this becoming a regular tradition for foreign pilgrims. By the end of the 12th century, an estimated half a million people walked the Camino in Europe out of a population of around 70 million at the time — the equivalent of approximately 5 million pilgrims if the same proportion of Europeans walked today. Much like today, merchants and hotels were abundant in exploiting this popularity for financial gain. This boost in the golden age of the Camino's popularity is owed in no small part to Pope Callixtus II, who put forth the idea of the Compostelan Holy Year — a year when St James' Day (the 25th of July) falls on a Sunday. Pilgrims making the journey at that time will have almost certainly referred to the Codex Calixtinus, an anthology and guidebook published around 1140, the 5th book of which has long been considered the world's oldest guidebook and basis for modern guidebooks, taking in cities such as Burgos, Leon and Astorga. It is probably due to this manuscript being primarily attributed to a French scholar named Aymeric Picaud that most pilgrimages began in France, resulting in the French Way becoming the best and most supported route to Santiago. While the French may consider theirs the unofficial primary way, the Spanish consider the Pyrenees Mountains, which border France and Spain, to be the starting point. Notwithstanding, it would be unfair to discount the Portuguese route, which can begin in Porto or Lisbon, first used by pilgrims to avoid the dangerous Muslim occupied regions of northern Spain during the middle ages. While the French route, crossing the Pyrenees, is the most popular and best supported, it is not the oldest. That accolade goes to the Camino Primitivo, which begins in the Spanish city of Oviedo, around a 90-minute drive north of Leon. These pilgrims were under the care and protection of both Catholic and Royal orders but travelled under near-constant threat. Walking for months or years at a time, contending with injury, illness, starvation and thieves, hoping for but a chance to stand in the main square of Compostela before the great cathedral in which the remains of St James were to be found, laying their weary hands on the stone pillar in the doorway to the point where it is visibly worn away.

The system of self-punishment to atone for one's sins, known as penance, was another reason for pilgrims to walk The Way. The Church encouraged the journey as a way for sinners to absolve themselves and thus ensure their place in heaven. This tradition lives on in Flanders, where one prisoner is released every year — provided that they walk the Camino with a heavily-laden backpack. Along with myself, that prisoner would be among the estimated 200,000 that travelled the Camino in

2014. As our medieval counterparts would have, some will even walk barefoot or ride horseback. The remaining walkers usually complete the route for the sport or the physical challenge, but I'm sure plenty of people do it simply because it is there. Whichever popular way you take, unique hostels for pilgrims, known as albergues or refugios, are prolific and closely resemble modern youth hostels. A night's stay (of which you can only take one) costs around 10 euros, and you can stay as long as you like the following day as long as you are out by eight. Most hostels are privately owned and are usually more expensive due to better amenities and in contrast the municipal hostels run by the local authority tend to be cheaper albeit somewhat basic.

Suppose you were to search the possessions of any random pilgrim: in that case, you are almost sure to find the pilgrim's passport or credential that I mentioned earlier. These are purchased from virtually anywhere on the route, although the vast majority of pilgrims will have already gained possession of one before they even set foot on the trail. The pass entitles the bearer to heavily discounted or free overnight accommodation and meals. Each pilgrim can hand over the passport at almost any hostel, hotel, restaurant, or church to be stamped, which serves as proof of the holder's journey, qualifying them to receive their Compostela — the certificate of completion of the Camino. Any pilgrim wishing to obtain a Compostela at the end of their Camino needs to have walked a minimum of 100km, and it is probably for this reason that many pilgrims choose Sarria as a starting point for their walk, as its bus and rail connections make it a logical starting point for those wishing to walk the minimum required distance. A pilgrims office volunteer will examine the passport to ensure qualification and ask the pilgrim their reasons for walking. After arriving in Santiago and collecting the Compostela, the pilgrims are welcome to attend one of the twice-daily pilgrim masses, where it is possible to have one's arrival announced.

Always somewhat of a history buff, I decided to do some research on The Way beforehand, and the modern history of the Camino makes for interesting reading. After dwindling numbers of pilgrims making the journey to Santiago over the centuries, the revival of the Camino in its modern incarnation can in no small part be attributed to a Galician priest and scholar named Elías Valiña Sampedro. Credited with creating one of the Camino's most recognisable symbols, the painted yellow arrow, Don Elias published a doctoral thesis on The Way while studying in Salamanca in 1965 and when he began the arduous task of re-marking long stretches of the Camino in the late 1970s, much of the Way was impassable. Undeterred, Don Elias enlisted an army of mayors and parish leaders in helping him establish a marked original route leading to Santiago, using an iconic yellow painted arrow. It is hard to imagine that a symbol, so synonymous with helping countless pilgrims to navigate The Way, can thank a Citroen GS for carrying the priest the entire length of the French Way, getting out only to hastily daub an arrow before continuing. One might think yellow to be an arbitrary choice of colour, but this is not the case. While an obvious choice in terms of visibility, yellow was also the colour of hiking trails in Don Elias' native Galicia. Plus, it also turned out the guy happened to have a shit-load of yellow paint lying around. Now, you might imagine a priest driving around painting yellow arrows in the direction of a religious place of interest would garner a certain amount of attention — and you'd be correct, it did. During one such incident, civil guards from the Spain/France border naturally asked what on earth he was doing, to which Don Elias quipped, "Preparing a great invasion from France!" Rather sportingly, the guards gave him time to explain himself further, albeit not until after his arrest. So arguably, the renaissance of the Camino de Santiago may never have occurred were it not for an old Citroen, a ton of yellow paint, and one of the most influential priests you've probably never heard of.

Don Elias ultimately published his pilgrim guide to the Camino trail in 1982, and (thanks in no small part to Pope John Paul II visiting Santiago the same year) almost 2000 pilgrims received their Compostela. This remarkable achievement did not go unnoticed for Don Elias as, in 1985, he was assigned to oversee the coordination of all the resources of the Way. Soon, albergues and refugios sprang up to coincide with his creative 'yellow arrow' solution. All this caught the eye of UNESCO, who declared Santiago de Compostela a world heritage site later that year and a place on the premiere European Cultural Itinerary in 1985. The Camino Frances or French Way became a world heritage site in its own right in 1993, since when pilgrim numbers have gone up substantially. Here are the numbers for fans of statistics;

1986	2,491
1989	5,760
1993	99,439
1999	154,613
2004	179,944
2010	272,000+

It is worth bearing in mind that these numbers do not include all visits to Santiago for the sole intention of venerating St James (i.e. those who didn't walk there), which peaked at a staggering 12 million in the last holy year of 2010. But, without Don Elias or modern inventions such as the internet, it isn't without question that The Way may have disappeared altogether. One needs to simply consider how different the Camino was before Don Elias. Linda Davidson and David Gitlitz made nearly half a dozen pilgrimages between the mid-seventies and nineties while accompanying medieval history students. During their first, in 1974, they remarked not meeting a single other pilgrim, followed by a massive increase in 1979, when they met one — a second World War veteran from France.

Don Elias died at the relatively young age of 60 in 1989, shortly before Pope John Paul's second visit to Santiago, and is buried along the Camino Frances in the tiny village of O Cebreiro, where his nephew Jose Valina is a shop owner across from the Basilica of Santa Maria Real, where his illustrious uncle's gravesite can be found near a statue paying tribute to the man. Apparently, Jose was following his uncle's footsteps closer than he realised because, after getting a flat tyre in Navarra, about 20km south of Pamplona, he was approached by a man who remarked once seeing a priest driving a Citroen having a similar misfortune some years previously. Since Don Elias died in the middle of his complete mapping of the route, his nephew felt compelled to carry the mantle, enlisting the help of British historian Laurie Dennett to continue the project.

Like our musician, I would be walking the best supported, most popular route to Santiago, the Camino Frances. Planning for the trip was well underway before I learned how many alternate routes were out there. For example, the only other routes to hold a place on the World Heritage list are the Routes of Northern Spain, of which there are four main ones. Now, when I say 'route', I am referring to a starting point, as many 'Ways' either diverge from or converge to other routes, such as the Frances. The list of possible routes to Santiago become countless if one considers every instance an established path splits. For example, the Camino Primitivo breaks away from the Camino Norte at Villaviciosa before joining the Camino Frances for the last 40km to Santiago. This is even before we look at historical starting points, such as the Aragonese, English or Irish ways.

Camino Frances

As I just mentioned, the French Way is by far the most popular route for pilgrims walking to Santiago. So-called because it begins (just about) in France before crossing the Pyrenees, after which a 780km walk awaits. The unofficial starting point is Saint-Jean-Pied-de-Port, although paths originate from other French cities such as Tours and Vézelay before joining the major artery at Saint-Jean. Pilgrims taking this route will pass through major cities such as Burgos, Leon, and Pamplona as many smaller Caminos eventually join up with the Frances.

Camino Portugués

Second, only in popularity to the French Way, the Portuguese Way (also known as the Coastal Way) has the option of starting in Porto from where one can follow the Douro River north into Spain, ending in Santiago via Padron. At just under 230km, it is significantly shorter than the over 600km option of beginning in the Portuguese capital of Lisbon, which includes the chance to visit the Alcobaça Monastery, a former medieval albergue. The Portuguese Way rose to prominence during the so-called Age of Discovery in the 15th century, and the route branches out into two shortly after leaving Porto — one continuing along urbanised beach paths popularised by German pilgrims, with the other proceeding centrally. After the two trails converge, the Portuguese Way crosses the Minho river into Spain at Tui, where a 110km march north to Santiago awaits.

Camino del Norte

The Camino del Norte (or Northern Way) consists of a whopping 820km hike through the Basque country, beginning at Irún on the French border before travelling along Spain's northern coast. Pilgrims travel part of the way along the Via Agrippa, an old Roman road used by medieval pilgrims when the Camino Frances became too dangerous during the Muslim occupation of Spain. Passing through Bilbao and Oviedo, the Norte eventually joins the Frances a couple of days' walk from Santiago. If seafood and beaches are your scene, perhaps the Camino Norte is the one for you. The Norte promises to take in an unrivalled view of 'Green Spain', which runs parallel to the French Way before meeting it in Arzua.

Camino Primitivo

Strangely, the oldest pilgrim route is the least popular in terms of pilgrim numbers. Believed to be the path taken by the original pilgrim, Alfonso II, in 814, the Camino Primitivo takes one from Oviedo to the area formerly known as Mount Libredon on which Santiago was built. While not experiencing the same footfall as the other routes, the Camino Primitivo has remained popular to some pilgrims due to that very fact. The crowds one can expect on the French Way are unheard of, with less than 5% of pilgrims surveyed in 2016 having taken this route to Santiago.

For any numberphiles out there, here are a few Camino facts and figures. Feel free to put these in a chart — pie or bar is fine. As you might expect, there isn't much between the genders — in the last holy year (2010), 272,412 pilgrims received their Compostela from the pilgrim office in

Santiago, with male pilgrims leading their female counterparts 55% to 45% with just under half of the total figure being of Spanish nationality. I was also somewhat shocked to learn that 12% of pilgrims receiving a Compostela did so having reached Santiago by bicycle, causing me to imagine leaping into bushes to avoid becoming road-kill to a lycra-clad team of professional cyclists. The remaining pilgrims walked, although a comparative handful completed The Way by horse (and even a few by wheelchair). Somewhat paradoxically, I would find myself in both the whopping 70% of pilgrims that walked the Camino Frances, as well as the mere 12% who started the journey at the supposed start of that route, St Jean-Pied-De-Port. I also (barely) fell into the 28% of pilgrims that walked any path under the age of 30, with more than half of the pilgrims in 2010 being between the ages of 30 and 60. Unsurprisingly, there is no official data on the dropout rate mid-Camino, leading me to believe either nobody does so, or if they do, don't tell anyone about it.

A few weeks before my intended start date, my wife and I hosted a dinner party for a few friends, during which the topic of my walking inevitably came up in conversation. It wasn't long before the discussion descended into that infinite loop of "Why?" that anyone who has spent an extended period of time with a toddler inevitably falls into. Rather disconcertingly, I found myself without a satisfactory answer. Why was I doing this? I wondered inwardly. Was I being reckless? Crazy even? I wanted to discover what kind of person undertakes this walk, so I dug a little deeper. Unsurprisingly, since The Way is, after all, a pilgrimage to kneel at the remains of a Saint, religious or spiritual reasons for walking came in at the top spot at 21%, but I was surprised to learn that over 17% of pilgrims questioned gave exercise as their main reason for walking. While plodding away on a treadmill seems infinitely more boring than taking in a historic pilgrimage route, it seemed like a disproportionate number of people who decided not to simply join a gym. Just 14% said their lust for adventure sent them walking to Santiago — a proportion I was sure would have been higher than those seeking a workout. The same percentage of pilgrims were quoted as walking The Way as a means of finding peace and relaxation from a vacation. Around a fifth of those receiving a Compostela attributed a social or cultural drive behind their reason to tackle the Way, with just under 10% seeing it as a 'chance of a lifetime' type deal.

In conclusion, virtually no one person walked the Camino for one single reason. When boiled down, there are as many reasons for walking as there are pilgrims, and no one reason can reasonably be judged to be worth more than any other. I would consider myself somewhat of an average pilgrim, walking for every reason, but also none of them. Reading up on all these statistics made me feel pretty insignificant, so I am at this moment declaring myself to be the only left-handed person named Duncan to ever walk the Camino Frances in the month of June. Now this book might be worth something.

So that was the how. Next was the when. I knew that I didn't want to rush this trip, so I decided to take two months off work to walk the Camino at my own pace. I didn't anticipate a problem regarding a leave of absence, mainly because my employers had been fantastic when I was assaulted, allowing me to have as much time as I needed, on full pay, until I felt ready to return to work. In addition, I was planning to walk in June and July, which are usually the time of the year when the workload is generally at its lightest for our company. As expected, I was granted the time off and wished a fond farewell. I haven't had such a great boss since I was self-employed, I thought.

3

LEARNING TO WALK

IIIIIIIIIIIIIIIIIIIIIIIIIIIIIIIIIIIIIIIIIIIIIIIIIIIIIIIIIIIIIIIIIIIIIIIIIIIIIIIIIIIIIIIIIIIIIIIIIII

MY FIRST EXPERIENCE of Spain was a disappointing package holiday on the Costa Blanca as a lad of fourteen, followed by a post A-Level week of debauchery five years later. The intervening years until the time of this writing have seen me make a steady transition from 24-hour partying to 2 to 4-hour functioning. With Club 18–30 shenanigans firmly in the rearview mirror of my life, I reasoned that the chance of witnessing a Glaswegian stag party doing shots out of each other's arse cracks would be vanishingly small on Camino. At almost 30, the whole endeavour probably appeared outwardly like some sort of pre-midlife crisis, one last adventure before I was undeniably on the path to middle age. To tell the truth, I wasn't looking forward to the milestone of three decades on this planet, but I wasn't exactly dreading it. I had no idea how the day itself might unfold, but the bookies' favourite saw me sitting in my underwear on the couch, drinking champagne straight out of the bottle with one of those curly plastic straws like some sort of eccentric millionaire. But enough stalling; some concrete plans for the Camino must be made.

Years ago, my wife and I did one of those bushcraft survival weekends where you learn all that outdoorsy stuff like making rope from nettle stems and rubbing sticks together to start a fire. Although I still had plenty of kit from that time, it was immediately apparent that I was going to need quite a bit more, so I quickly researched the equipment I thought I might need on such a trip and was pleasantly surprised to learn that most guidebooks warn pilgrims that they are more likely to have a problem from over-packing than under. I had the type of backpack, clothes and walking boots that I needed from previous camping trips, which only left a torch, an electric razor, mosquito repellent, medicine, a first aid kit, a notebook (in which to keep a diary of my adventures), a penknife, a USB phone charger a water bottle and a guidebook to buy. While I enjoy a Bear Grylls adventure as much as the next man, it didn't seem likely I would have to gut a snake or hide my excrement from predators. What does he know anyway? He isn't even a real bear.

The list of things I needed gave me a headache, so I went for a lie-down — which only reminded me that I also needed a pillow and a blanket. As I stared vacantly at the ceiling, thoughts of something unfortunate happening to me began to form in my mind. What if I got lost or injured? I do get injured easily, even managing to crash an exercise bike once. What if some malady, however unlikely, were to strike me down? My ever-racing mind caused me to spend more hours than I care to admit researching every illness that could befall a man my age. If you were thinking of looking up how to predict a brain aneurysm, I could save you some time — you can't. I was starting to look forward to this trip a little less.

With the list of equipment I was going to need steadily rising, I embarked to a local branch of a well-known UK retailer of outdoor products, which (for potential legal reasons that I can't be bothered to research) I will call Proceed Outside. Now, before you even get inside the building, you must navigate your way through a small tent city, not unlike the ones you might see on Skid Row, as you pass canvas bargains left and right. I have been camping on several occasions but have never seen so many tents in one place — with styles and sizes to suit all budgets, from tent mansions including receptions and drawing rooms to simple pop-up one-man efforts. Bravely I ventured indoors to see what stupid shit I could fill it with first. The previous week, I discussed my upcoming trip with a colleague whose father had walked the Camino twice and brought a tent and sleeping bag twice before sending both home early on each occasion. While none of the tents were in any serious danger of being bought, it somehow felt rude walking past them without appreciating them erected in all their splendour, no doubt something I would fail to achieve with aplomb.

I am confident that anyone reading this would guess that the knife cabinet would be my first stop inside bricks and mortar. Various types of bushcraft and hunting knives were on display before me, separated by a (hopefully) locked sliding glass door. Previous scenarios that couldn't have been further from my mind were suddenly at the forefront; Could I end up needing a knife? Should I assume that animal/pilgrim attacks were inevitable? Would I get on The Way to find pilgrims huddled around hostel bedrooms comparing knives, leaving me shunned for being the only pilgrim without one? Since even the cheapest option was north of £100, I decided ridicule for the lack of a knife would be a risk I would have to take. With that thought not long out of my head, I continued along the aisle to find another cabinet filled with sophisticated navigation systems for me to consider, whereupon I pondered the use of such a device should I become lost on my way to Saint James (somewhat prophetic as you may discover should you decide to read on). I was already familiar with the painted yellow arrows designed to keep walkers on the trail, but there is no way you can convince me that a pilgrim of centuries past wouldn't choose a £300 GPS smartwatch that (possibly) wishes you a *Buen Camino!* on command. And it would be well used, as I have an almost mythical status as someone who can quickly become lost getting to and around places he frequents. Should anyone ever conceive of a World's Worst Navigator Award, it would surely be a foregone conclusion that I would win, resulting in the World's Greatest Son mug I received at age 10 having a serious contender for its pride of place on mum's mantlepiece.

The only part of my walking 'career' worth mentioning is the section of the Trans Pennine Way between my house in Warrington to that of my parents in Altrincham that my wife and I walked once a year on Good Friday. Although much shorter in comparison, I still considered myself physically fit enough to meet the challenge of walking much further on a daily basis. Until this point, I had solely considered The Way to be a walk — by which I mean only walking is involved. I was aware that the Pyrenees mountains must be conquered but was confident no actual climbing would be involved. This didn't stop me from being pulled towards the vast array of climbing gear on offer or even risking embarrassment by attempting to try it on. Still, the nauseating prices at everything I had looked at so far meant I would have to risk becoming lost finding a mountain that I would be ill-equipped to climb. All while unarmed. By this point, the list of stuff I wouldn't need or couldn't afford was taking up almost all of my time in the store. I quickly disregarded this, however, and moved on to something even more useless to me — fishing gear. Large bodies of water were going to be few and far between, but I imagined myself, (fishing) rod in hand, catching my dinner like those people who know what they are doing.

The shopping trip continued along its steady descent into the ridiculous given the context of my visit. A bedside lamp? Shelving units?

An inflatable sofa? At what point does it cease to be camping, but just a case of taking all of your crap to a field? Perhaps I could save even more money catching fish in my mouth like a bear or even trawl for them in one of those massive dinghies that would be more at home in the RNLI fleet. Worrying about the expense of this trip whilst simultaneously trying to keep my pack under the recommended 10 kilos I found to be the general consensus in online forums, the notion was simply laughable if I took everything I *might* use.

As I made my way to a large clearing in the middle of the store, my eyes fell upon the array of grills that could be mine if I wanted to lose a couple of grand, not to mention my mind. I gave a short exhalation through the nostrils at the imagined sight of myself cooking one of those comically large steaks you only see in cartoons as a means of sustaining myself towards the approximate 50,000 required calories for walking The Way. Adjacent to the display, a colourful array of camping meals caught my eye. Perhaps I should forgo the extra change of clothes in favour of assaulting my digestive system with a shepherd's pie that possesses the ability to heat itself, I mused. I was more intrigued by the science over the potential taste and, after much Googling, I learned the meals are, in fact, kits containing several components, usually a varying combination of iron, magnesium powder, salt, and water. When the contents of the water pouch are poured over the included heater pad, enough heat (approximately 100 degrees Fahrenheit) is released to safely warm up a pre-cooked meal in around 10 minutes. For your convenience, I have compiled a step-by-step guide on the preparation of a meal system that I have neither purchased nor tasted. You're welcome.

1.   Obtain permission from your spouse to buy one.
2.   Tear open the heater bag.
3.   Place the meal in the bag against the heater pad.

4. Pour the saltwater pouch into the bag to start the heating
    process.
5. Fold the opening over and secure the bag closed.
6. Place the meal in the heater bag on a heat-safe surface.
7. Throw the meal in the bin because it was disgusting.

Okay, maybe not that last one, but after the camping gear distraction,
I decided it was high time for me to look at the clothing — something I
knew I needed. This was in no small part due to how irked my wife was
becoming. I knew this partly because it is something you become attuned
to after so many years together and partly because she outright told me.

Because I already owned them from much wimpier expeditions, I felt
able to disregard the heavy-duty walking boot and backpack required
which, to my mind, was 99% of what I needed, but quickly decided the
remaining 1% was going to have to also include a torch, a pair of sandals,
a portable phone charger, a bandana, and a couple of pairs of some
fetching quick-drying pants that could transform into shorts courtesy
of a zip below the knee. Buried somewhere in my spare room that
resembled a charity shop intake, I already had a waterproof jacket for
myself, and although severely tempted, decided against purchasing a
matching horse raincoat on prominent display, mainly because it would
be the height of summer and therefore highly unlikely my hypothetical
horse would need it. Of course, there was the camo gear for the pilgrim
wishing to remain unseen (beside hi-vis versions for those desiring the
total opposite), although I struggled to picture myself sneaking up on
prey/enemy pilgrims, no matter how fun it sounded. Thermal gear was
something I also considered briefly as my own were somewhat tattered
before I remembered again that I would be walking in temperatures only
marginally cooler than the surface of the sun. So into the 'maybe' pile
they went. The next stop was the sleeping bags, but since there wouldn't

be a tent between myself and the stars, there probably wouldn't be a sleeping bag either. Then again, I could lose my remaining marbles and become one of the approximately 20,000 pilgrims to cycle the Way each year and buy a new bike, ship it to the start line at great expense, and probably commence my search for a new wife after my current one divorces me for spending such an amount. I already felt like I was spending a fortune just standing there.

Apparently, to the allegedly trained eye, my dithering can easily be mistaken as needing assistance. At least this was the only sensible conclusion at which I could arrive, as a cherub-faced assistant shuffled awkwardly beside us in an apparent attempt to calm our fears about buying suitable clothes for hiking — and boy, was that a weight off my mind.

"Do you need any help?" he whispered, seemingly for the first time in his life due to his glaring lack of confidence. Now I would not be considered tall at a decidedly average 5′9″, but I was at least a clear head above this lad who looked as if he was drowning in his uniform due to it being comically oversized, as if he had swapped roles with a giant older sibling in some kind of bet.

"Thank God!" I exclaimed as I held up the quick-drying hiking trousers. "Do you have these in an extra medium?"

He turned to head towards what I assumed to be the warehouse area before stopping as the confusion took hold. In the corner of my eye, I could see my wife's hand and forehead meet in apparent embarrassment at my unsolicited dad joke. His mouth opened, but no sound had a chance to escape before I sped off, feigning excitement at the first thing that caught my eye.

"Oh look, gilets!" I enthused." (ˈʒɪleɪ, ˈʒiːleɪ/ *noun;* a light sleeveless padded jacket) For when my arms are warm but my body is cold — genius!"

When I was sure I was not being followed, I slowed to find myself amongst travel-ready gadgets of all sizes and budgets. I have no idea how they work, but it is apparently possible to get a TV and WiFi signal while on the move. So I moved on to look elsewhere. And by elsewhere, I mean back home immediately, unless I "wanted to walk home", as my wife put it before marching straight for the exit.

Later that evening, I practised carefully laying out my entire kit before packing and unpacking it all over and over. After much practice, I was able to do the whole thing in under 10 swear words. In all, I was going to be carrying the following. Take a moment to study this list carefully and try to find the red herrings.

Quick drying convertible pants x 2
Travel Journal
Earplugs
Camino guide book
Electric razor
European power adapter
False moustache
Bandana x 2
Quick-drying towel
Portable phone charger
Walking Boots
Travel washing line
Gilet (with detachable hood)*
Sandals
Pair of socks x 4
A gun
Underwear x 3 (x 4 if you count the pair I was currently wearing)
Assorted Travel toiletries

A money belt
Sunglasses
T-Shirts x 3
Suncream
Walking pole

*I bought the gilet by the Way — if I was going to get lost, I would at least look stylish while I did so.

4

LAST OF THE SUMMER WHINE

||||||||||||||||||||||||||||||||||||||||||||||||||||||||||||||||||||||||||||||||||||||||||||||||||||||||||||||||||||||||||||||||||||||||||||||||||||||||||

WHEN I WAS in secondary school, I had an English teacher named Mr Hamish. A strange sort of fellow, he once threatened to give me detention if I didn't tell him how to get past a section of *Resident Evil* he was stuck on after pulling me out in the middle of a physics lesson to do so. In an apparent protest at the school administration due to his use of the 'N' word (in the context of a discussion centring around Mark Twain), he wore a custom-made baseball cap to a class that read, "I'm not prejudiced, I hate everyone." That message always stuck with me, and I have used it often if I ever feel the need to justify my wish to ignore the company of others. Ever since I conceived the idea of making this journey, I was in no doubt that if I walked the Camino, I would do so alone with unashamedly selfish reasoning. Not only does too much time in the company of other people drive me to the cusp of madness at times, but I also did not want at any point to feel obligated to change my intended plans to suit anyone else's. I was going to walk when I wanted, for as long as I wanted, and stop when I wanted. I very much doubt anyone would even take someone as bad-tempered as me for a walking companion anyway. Nobody even likes to watch movies with me due to my habit of pointing out every mistake I see. For some strange reason, people don't want to hear why their favourite film is crap.

I knew there was no going back now, and I booked my plane ticket that evening. To be safe, I booked with a particular budget airline famous for denying refunds as if it was going out of fashion, leaving me no option to chicken out. Whilst admiring more fancy, unnecessary kit online, I happened upon an article about the "danger" that any of the handful of stray dogs might pose to myself or others during the Camino. I wasn't particularly anxious about a possible encounter but was going to be sure to take heed of the warning to avoid feeding them anyway since I was in no great want to have a four-legged companion for a stage or two. I, therefore, refrained from taking animal repellent, but one superfluous item I was going to afford myself was my GoPro camera (housed in its practically indestructible and waterproof case), which was to be strapped to my body so that I could make a point-of-view type film that I could cut together to show off my adventure to enraptured friends. I assumed if people wanted to see anything, they would probably rather it be a two-minute film instead of an endless slideshow of poorly-framed camera phone pictures. I settled into the last night in my own bed for a while with a sense of nervous apprehension and fitful sleep at the thought of any number of things that could go wrong.

The closest airport in France to the start point of St Jean was Biarritz, and getting there would require flying from London Stansted — almost a four-hour drive from my home in Warrington. As we were leaving the house, my terrier, Arthur, seemed insistent that I, in particular, were to not leave the house. Of course, I wasn't about to take this at face value and proceeded to waste half an hour panicking that, after years of dim-wittedness, my dog had finally achieved some level of sentience and was now trying to warn me of a premonition he was having — almost certainly of my own untimely demise. After all, he had saved our lives on countless occasions from the postman or other dogs that had come anywhere near the house, something he was clearly doing now. After much dithering, my wife reminded me that Arthur once attacked his own reflection in a pond after mistaking it for another dog and suggested I was probably putting too much stock in his mental capacity. As I closed the front door behind me, I took comfort in the fact he had finally forgiven me for telling him he was adopted.

Before flying to France the next day, my wife and I decided to make a mini-vacation out of it and spend the night at a hotel adjacent to the main terminal. We had a lovely day followed by a pleasant evening despite that strange feeling of impending separation. Saturday night made way for Sunday morning, and it was time for me to kiss my wife goodbye and set off to the continent with a sense of reckless abandon. As we were about to part ways, she gave me a small pendant on which was the likeness of the patron saint of travellers, St Christopher. Etched on the back were the words, "Camino de Santiago 2014". With tears collecting in the corners of my eyes, I knew that I should have known she would have something like this up her sleeve to hasten the onset of emotion — she always does. My wife does get upset easily though, something that increased markedly a few years later during her pregnancy — on one occasion, calling me in tears because she found herself unable to blow up a balloon. It hadn't really occurred to me until that moment, but in our ten years together, we hadn't spent more than one or two days apart from one another. Ever since my "accident" (her preferred term for it), she has been terrified for my safety in everyday situations, never mind peculiar adventures in the Spanish wilderness. I knew that what happened to me was a terrible ordeal for my wife to go through, and as the thought of calling the whole thing off flashed across my mind, she had already read it. There was no way she was going to let me quit now after those "bastard M6 roadworks", so I kissed her one last time before joining the security queue — a queue entirely within eyesight of the general public I had just left behind. What followed was a fifteen-minute sequence of waving to each other as the distance between us increased at a snail's pace, and the humour of the situation was effective in helping me stay composed. The whole exchange was in stark contrast to virtually everyone else in my life after learning of my intention to embark on this trip, who fell into two camps — those who had heard of the Camino and didn't care I was doing it, and those who hadn't heard of the Camino and still didn't care I was doing it. I remember mentioning my impending trip in passing to a friend of my wife, who was dumbfounded at the concept of travelling abroad for the sole purpose of walking. Each explanation I offered was met with the same response, "But, I don't get it...." I haven't seen her since, but I do still wonder if "it" has ever been got.

Once I had made my way through security, I immediately felt self-conscious owing to my appearance. It had seemed perfectly sensible to dress how I intended to on my first step as a pilgrim until that moment. However, I now felt incredibly out of place in a departure lounge full of businessmen and sun-seeking families — as if a heartbroken explorer had accidentally wandered into a departure lounge. Be that as it may, the seed was sown. The die cast. It had proved to be a long journey from sitting at a desk watching another man's first day on the trail to me stepping my first as a pilgrim. This wasn't going to be like all the other times. But then again, I would say that, wouldn't I?

When I was a child, every day between the school bells signalling the end of one school year and the start of the next was spent in Ireland. As a result, I became well used to travelling on planes alone, but as I shuffled aimlessly amongst duty-free spirits and overpowering scents, it struck me that this was the first time I had done so since. I had no idea what to do with myself besides perusing the small number of shops in a manner that must have appeared shoplifter-ish to staff. After the announcement of a short delay to my flight, it eventually came time for me to queue up at the departure gate. After spending what felt like an eternity next to an east-facing plate glass window that magnified the heat of the sun bearing down on it, we gratefully began to board the aircraft. Conspicuous amongst us all were a well-dressed elderly couple, who seemed a little out of place to be flying on a budget airline. Attire aside, in a move of breath-taking decadence, they had printed their boarding pass using colour ink, and unlike every other passenger for this flight, stood in the queue designated "Priority boarding". To anyone who isn't familiar with this, allow me to describe it. You pay a surcharge to get the privilege of boarding the plane before anyone else, and your reward is sitting on the hot, uncomfortable plane for longer than you need to. However, Mr and Mrs Senior were mistaken as they had not, in fact, purchased such a priority and would now have to board after my fellow plebs and I, much to their chagrin. Despite this and, although I was at the front of the regular line, I still would have been happy to let them in front of me so we could all get to Biarritz a few seconds sooner. However, this would not do at all. The gentleman proceeded to argue his case to an unmoved and heavily pregnant member of staff until the point where all other passengers were safely in their seats, leaving him little choice other than to finally admit defeat and board long after the last of us. The incident amused more than a few, with the young man sitting beside me saying he would have gladly sat down on fresh hay instead of a seat just to see the look on their faces. Chuckling softly, I finally felt at ease towards the upcoming adventure I had spent the last two weeks preoccupied with. The flight was long, uncomfortable and boring in equal measure, but it landed safely and on time at a dreary and soulless Biarritz Airport.

Now, I live in the north of England where, most years, summer is just when the rain gets warmer, but stepping through the doors at Biarritz airport made me feel I was a Borrower opening the oven door to see how the big people's Sunday roast is coming along. Immediately I regretted wearing the gilet, and after 5 minutes was regretting wearing any clothes at all. As I stepped outside the terminal building to check the bus timetable to Bayonne, which was to be my resting place for the night, I could almost hear the sweat pumping out of my every pore. I was well on my way towards becoming Soylent Green jerky when I noticed that there were plenty of other pilgrims dotted around me. This made sense since we were at the nearest airport to the most common starting point of the most popular Camino route. Like birds of a feather, five or six of them eventually organised themselves awkwardly into a posse that was going to take an hour-long taxi ride to St-Jean-Pied-de-Port, kindly inviting me to join them. Since I had a hotel booked, I took the short ride to Bayonne and stayed there, heading to the start point in the morning and so politely declined. I never saw any of them again, but I often like to imagine that they completed their Camino together, becoming life-long best friends and getting into all manner of hilarious jams, perhaps even crossing into Santiago holding hands while they thought of me and what might have been.

The bus ride to Bayonne was much shorter than I anticipated , and I disembarked less than twenty minutes later, armed with a printed map of the immediate area for ease of finding my hotel. It turned out there was no need as my bed for the night was immediately adjacent to the same bus station from which I would travel to St Jean first thing in the morning. By the time I reached the hotel, I was dripping with sweat, despite having hardly walked a step outside as I dropped my bags down on the floor of my small yet well-appointed room before realising that I hadn't eaten all day. Instantly discovering myself to be ravenous, I demolished the minuscule bag of Haribo left on my pillow (a mint would probably be old-fashioned now, I suppose), barely able to contain myself to open the packet first. Pondering my next move, I watched a dozen or so men fly-fishing in the River Ardour through my room window before taking the first of many showers that day.

I am old enough to remember when Sunday was a day of rest for the most part. Pubs closed early, most shops were closed entirely, and people generally took it easy. Over the years, this structure has gradually been eroded to the point where Sunday is almost indistinguishable from the rest of the week retail-wise. So, imagine my surprise when I went out to discover the best of Bayonne, only to find that practically every bar, shop and restaurant is to be closed. After settling down in my room, I headed down to reception armed with high school French, where I asked the lady on duty where a hungry man might find a supermarket. She listened to my question with patience before responding with detailed instructions, which I was confident I understood, only to conclude with, "But it's closed today anyway." Hangry beyond the point of reason, I stepped into the heat in the direction of the town centre anyway.

On my way there, I happened across an Irish pub called Katy Daly's, where I couldn't resist stopping for a pint, cementing my assertion that no matter where in the world you go, the Irish will have scouted ahead and put up a pub for you. After I left the bar, I continued along in the same direction I was heading, happening upon Le Comptoir Irlandais, a chain of stores selling all manner of crap with varying combinations of the Irish tricolour, harp or shamrock on them. The store was, of course, closed because it was Sunday, denying me a hefty dose of tacky nostalgia. I continued on and eventually found a quaint family-run crepe restaurant called Creperie a la Bolee, where I ordered the house special crepe with some beautiful French lager to wash it down with. I was planning to abstain from alcohol altogether on this pilgrimage, but since I hadn't technically started yet, this one didn't count. And neither did the next two. The waitress was a charming lady who interrupted her own dinner before showing admirable restraint in holding back laughter when I attempted to order in French.

It was a beautiful day in a beautiful town and, despite some discomfort, I was determined to make the most of it. The streets were empty and quiet, and I very much enjoyed taking the chance to explore them. My bus was early the next morning, so I decided to head back to my room before night fell and my navigation skills became exponentially worse. I laid in bed and turned on the tiny television, soon falling asleep to the sound of the French football team trouncing Jamaica in their final warm-up game before heading out to Brazil for the upcoming World Cup. Allez les Bleus!

5
ON YOUR MARKS
||||||||||||||||||||||||||||||||||||||||||||||||||||||||||||||||||||||||||||||||||||

I GOT UP early the following day and stumbled downstairs to pick at the unattractive continental breakfast. I felt too tired and irritable to eat much and, after yawning my way through half a yoghurt and a piece of fruit, it was time to begin the soon-to-be daily ritual of packing my bag and getting a move on. I left the hotel, getting to the station about 15 mins before my bus' scheduled departure time of 7:45, leaving enough time to check I had everything at least two dozen times. I was confident that I was in the right place, not least because of all the people dressed like me, also carrying huge backpacks. The sun was already beating down, putting a powerful thirst on me, but I didn't dare drink anything in case I needed a piss halfway to St Jean — I've learned that one the hard way in the past. The bus meandered through some attractive French countryside and arrived in St Jean at around 9, at which time I made straight for my hotel for the evening, The Hotel Ramuntcho. A crudely drawn clock on a piece of paper pinned to the front desk let me know I was too early for check-in, so I instead busied myself by exploring the little town from which I was to take the longest walk of my life.

Only the French can name a town after a literal description and make it exotic to foreign ears. Perhaps the residents of Saint-John-at-the-Foot-of-the-Pass feel the same way when they look at a map of Britain and see places like Grimsby, but I somehow doubt it. Just under five miles from the Spanish border as the crow flies, Saint-Jean has that unique quality that makes a town feel like a village, with picturesque narrowing streets lined with traditional craft and food shops overlooking the river Nive. The cobbled Rue de la Citadelle is the main street leading from Porte St. Jacques to Porte d'Espagne via a stone bridge that crosses the river. As I walked from one side to the other, I took a moment on the bridge to enjoy the unexpected treat of the view of the balconied houses lining the water. As you approach the Porte d'Espagne, you will notice the 14th-century Gothic church originally built by Sancho the Strong to commemorate a significant victory over the occupying Moors, but was unfortunately not open to visitors on the day I was there.

As I made my way back towards the hotel, I noticed one of those delightful little tour busses made to look like a train and decided the €2 fee was probably worth it even though I had probably seen everything it was about to show me already. While this was true, the train also took us (by us, I mean just myself and the driver) up to the citadel overlooking the down, when several signs detailing Saint Jean's history gave some much-needed historical and architectural context.

In the Spring of 2010, I visited the glorious Lyme Park on the edge of the Peak District with my wife. Despite the dreary weather, we were looking forward to taking in some of the stunning views on the 1400 acre estate that was the setting for the 1995 BBC adaptation of Jane Austin's Pride and Prejudice. After parking the car, we made our way through turnstiles into what probably was once some kind of farmhouse to pay the admission. It wasn't cheap at £13.50 each to gain entry into the house and garden, but we had driven a reasonably long way to get there, so we bit the bullet and paid.

We were welcomed by a woman in her mid to late forties, wearing a most unnaturally friendly smile with nothing behind the eyes. Think Christian Bale in *American Psycho*.

"Hello, welcome to Lyme Park." She soothed, positively human-like.

"Hi!" My wife chirped. "How much is it for the house and garden?" She added even though we already knew.

"Well, it's £13.50 each..." She leaned forward as if about to dispense sordid gossip. "...but if you join the National Trust, it works out to be less than £10 for both of you."

She stood up straight, probably expecting gasps.

I was aware that the National Trust offered memberships but had never purchased one because the infrequency we visited National Trust properties did not make it worthwhile.

"No thanks." I said politely, raising my hand, "We just...."

She cut me off, pretending she didn't hear me.

"And if you join the trust, you get free entry into over 500 National Trust properties."

"I know," I retorted, "We only want to visit one. This one."

Undeterred, she pressed on, "You also get a handbook, newsletters, and a magazine sent to you three times a year."

My eyes narrowed.

She snapped her head to face my wife, convinced I was too stupid to realise how stupid I was being and that my stupidity was keeping me from seeing what a stupidly-good deal I was passing up.

"And free parking is included when you join the trust."

When she registered that my wife was unmoved by her hard sell, her left eye began twitching. She was making the National Trust sound like the National Front.

"But you're saving £3.50!" She blurted at last. "Don't you *want* to save these places for future generations?"

At this point, I wouldn't have taken a membership even if it was free.

"If I take a membership for £10 a month, I'm not saving £3.50. I'm spending £120."

Mercifully, a senior staff member sensed the growing unease and spirited her out of the room, hopefully for a factory reset. Anecdotally, I have heard that volunteers have a far more aggressive approach to sales than paid employees. After the Battle of Lyme Park, I am minded to agree.

Maddening upselling tactics were fortunately absent from the Camino, with the closest thing to bureaucracy being the pilgrim office on the edge of St Jean. Somewhat out of character, I managed to find the pilgrim office quite easily, probably due to the greater concentration of hikers gathered around it. Just a two-minute walk down the same cobbled street as my hotel and adjacent to the famous Spanish gates, I stepped inside to see a large room with a long table on the left-hand side over which an elderly man and woman were leaning, pouring over maps with a couple of flustered-looking pilgrims. There were no other walkers that I could see, so I occupied myself until it was my turn by leafing over pamphlets or studying posters, almost all of which was a warning for the reader to be ready for changeable weather when crossing the Pyrennees, something I was to do tomorrow. In the corner of the office was a giant bucket filled with rain ponchos of all kinds, with a small bi-lingual sign inviting anyone in want of such a thing to help themselves. I wondered whether the people who left theirs there were either confident in their prediction of the weather or had simply packed too many. Eventually, I was seen by a lovely English woman called Nora while her husband, Eric, was still struggling to make himself understood to the same foreign pilgrims as when I arrived. Nora explained to me that she and Eric had fallen in love with Saint-Jean several years after first arriving there to walk their own Camino and several trips later wished to give back by volunteering, now that their ageing limbs would allow no more pilgrimages. After gratefully accepting Nora's offer for a cup of tea, I paid my fee of €10 to receive my Camino scallop shell, a written description of what to expect on my first day's walk to Roncesvalles (including helpful information on terrain and elevation) and my all-important pilgrim passport. The pilgrim passport (sometimes referred to as a credential) is a folded piece of card that looks like some kind of toy passport one might use to amuse a child, into which I would receive stamps proving that I was really passing through the places between here and Santiago. I completed a short questionnaire concerning my reasons for walking and, after assuring her I was prepared for the rain that may or may not fall during my maiden voyage, I bid farewell to the "Ames du Chemin de Saint-Jacques" or the "Friends of the Way of Saint James" to look at my new literature in greater detail in my (hopefully) available hotel room. On the way there I noticed a special offer at the small convenience store that offered a 'Camino packed lunch' for only 10 euros. Consisting of a sandwich, a packet of crisps and a drink, I baulked at the price, particularly since I felt less than confident purchasing a sandwich when I didn't know what came between the bread beforehand. Since I have a child's self-discipline when it comes to eating while on holiday, I instead settled on a packet of chocolate biscuits.

I arrived back at the hotel to find the front desk staffed by a gentleman in his late 50s. I stepped up to the counter, expecting him to look up and check me in, but he did neither. What followed was well over a minute of standing before him, watching on as he carefully studied one of those old-fashioned ledger books more at home in a period drama. Unsure what to do next, I gently cleared my throat, after which he briefly looked up before resuming his bookkeeping. Upon this, I rather less subtly hoisted my bag on the counter next to him, fished out my passport and set it down in his direct eye line. Beside him on the counter was a small sign on which the Union Jack could be seen amongst various other flags — something I can only assume is there to represent the languages ignored at that hotel. He checked me in using the fewest number of words possible, causing a chuckle from the person who now stood behind me. I glanced back to see a young lady rather amused by our exchange, almost certainly mistaking it for a sort of street theatre. Later that evening at dinner, a lady I assumed to be Madame Fawlty was every bit the conversational black hole as her husband when she unenthusiastically recommended the Basque Chicken for dinner. I tried some jovial conversation but quickly became exhausted as I wondered what she and her husband talked about in bed after a night painting the town beige. In all fairness, I would be remiss if I didn't compliment whichever of them cooked the chicken, as it was simply exquisite. I dined alone in the hotel restaurant, with my only visitor being an elderly spaniel named Lola, who sat beside me briefly before disappearing. With no human waiting staff at hand, I stood up to leave, at which point the lady of the house appeared out of nowhere to strongly advise me to make my breakfast order now, as no one would be there in the morning to take it. Labelled meals would be laid out in the hotel restaurant for patrons to collect.

"Can I see the breakfast menu please?" I asked.

She rolled her eyes and reached under the desk, groping blindly for a few seconds, before pulling out a single sheet of A4. I took it from her, noticing immediately that the menu contained only one item listed in four different languages. It turns out one can have anything they like at the Hotel Ramuntcho as long as it is the 'express breakfast'.

"I think I'll have the express breakfast," I uttered with feigned indecision.

She snatched the 'menu' back from me before making a note in her ledger of doom before leaving the room in what turned out to be our last interaction.

"Merci beaucoup," I said to the space her miserable face used to occupy.

I took some time in the hotel bar to become acquainted over drinks with a small group of pilgrims from Scotland — most notably Trevor and Leanne, a married couple who were planning to walk for a week, and Derek, a parish priest from Dundee, doing the same. An hour turned into three before my head hit the pillow. So much for getting a good night's rest.

6

DON'T STOP WALKING

‖‖

IT JUST SO happened that I chose to begin this Camino on my wife's birthday. She had known I would be gone for a good while and enjoyed teasing me with mock morose how lonely she would be without me on this of all days. I was disappointed not to be with her to celebrate, more so than if it had been my own birthday. Freezing my bollocks off at the crack of dawn, I called to wish her many happy returns, at which time I felt something I rarely had, if ever, felt before. I was homesick.

What the fuck was I doing?

It was far too late to start asking stupid questions, so I quickly stifled the thought and went back inside to make my final preparations. I threw the 'express' breakfast that had been laid out carefully for me in the dining room down my neck, choosing it carefully from half a dozen identical ones belonging to unseen guests. Then, at precisely 7 am on the 10th of June 2014, I officially became a pilgrim and set off into the French dawn with reckless abandon.

Shortly after setting off down the cobbled street, somewhere between the Spanish gate and the pilgrim bridge, I felt a dull pain in my left knee as the southern French drizzle fell over me like pins and needles. Surely this wasn't going to end in injury — a problem I had not expected with 499.9 miles left to go but, as I found my stride, the ache melted away before I was even out of the town limits. Almost at once, I observed how steep the initial climb was from the off and, to counter the 10kg bag on my back, I needed to lean forward so much that I was almost using my hands to help me walk, in much the same way a primate would. When I looked ahead into the distance to find an object to focus on moving towards, they seemed to get no closer. The Pyrenees Mountains were mocking me.

I reached the fencepost. More hill. I made it round the corner. More hill. I made it past the grove of trees. More hill. I didn't dare turn around in case that was now uphill. In the end, a welcome distraction from the neverending incline appeared in the form of the first person I had seen since setting off from my hotel. It was a farmer trundling along in his tractor, and the sight of him prompted me to remember that, just before leaving the pilgrim office, Nora had made a specific point to tell me to wave to any Basque farmers I might pass the next day as a sign of respect for passing through their land. I didn't know whether the road itself even was their land or a public highway, but a wave wasn't too much to ask either way. It appeared that this farmer was the first of many graduates from the same grumpy finishing school as my hoteliers the previous evening. Here is a short list of what I did not receive after waving to the half dozen I met during the following hour: a wave back, a thank you, a smile, a nod, a peace sign, a hat-tip or a thumbs up. The only people I had seen so far that day were farm hands with non-verbal communication skills that mostly involved staring at me vacantly as if I was an advert for junk mail. It was a strange feeling to not really meet anyone willing to go beyond this but, as time passed, the beauty of the rolling Basque countryside was company enough.

The tradition among pilgrims who come across each other (or anyone else for that matter) is to wish each other a "Buen Camino!", which is the basic equivalent of wishing one another a safe trip. Although I regularly saw other walkers, I hadn't said this to anyone else yet due to a childish fear of rejection or ridicule. Eventually, I plucked up the courage to say it to a young woman who was about to overtake me somewhere near the French-Spanish border. I looked to my side as she was passing and said, "Buen Camino!" only for her to say it at the exact same time, only slightly louder. Now I had a dilemma. Should I assume that she didn't hear me because she spoke louder than I did, thus risking myself to appear rude for not reciprocating? Or should I repeat myself even though she probably did hear me, possibly appearing to suffer from some kind of tic as a result? With too much time spent pondering my next move, I resolved to say nothing in future until other pilgrims did so first, after which I would reciprocate. But not too fast as to seem needy. Or too slow as to appear dim-witted. This was going to drive me mad before I was very much older.

During this initial stage, I noticed small piles of stones at several places along the road. Often they were accompanied by messages or poems on top of way markers or in the presence of a shrine such as a cross. No one seems to be certain of the reason for this; some suggest that it is merely a way of helping pilgrims stay on the path, while others theorise that the carrying of stones is a metaphor for the burdens we carry in life. Perhaps pilgrims are the type of people attracted to the idea of the permanence of a rock. In this way, they are leaving their mark, however small, that would last forever. Whatever the reason, I found myself keeping a stone in my pocket for a few miles, adding it precariously to the next pile I came across. As for my reasoning, I was only doing it because everyone else was.

After about two hours admiring chestnut trees and grazing cows between bouts of social awkwardness, I reached the Refuge Orisson, the first hostel since leaving St Jean. Standing around 100 metres before the building, I met an American man, who introduced himself as Jason from Hawaii. He was desperately trying to rearrange his backpack and, as we chatted, I realised why. Clutched in his hands was the largest glass jar of Nutella in the observable universe. Jason explained that he was eager to shed as much weight from his backpack as possible. He looked around the same height and weight as me but, by my estimate, was carrying at least double the weight on his back that I was. It had apparently dawned on him that his decision to bring a lifetime supply of hazelnut spread was probably ill-advised when you consider that you have to carry it up and down a mountain on day 1. I doubt that I was the first or last person to have this conversation with him that day, which was something I found funny but a little bit sad at the same time — a bit like a clown in the rain. After chatting with him for five minutes, three of which he spent trying to convince me to take the jar, I left him and headed inside the hostel. I would bump into Jason several times throughout the early stages of the Camino, with him never failing to appear more and more eccentric in each instance.

Although overnight accommodation was available at the Orisson, I hadn't been walking long, and it was still only around 9.30 in the morning, making it a wholly unsuitable place to rest for the night. However tempting, I wasn't about to admit defeat to the gradual chafing of my poorly fixed backpack straps that were beginning to win a war of attrition with my shoulders. The premises were warm, dry and comfortable, and the host was genial. I stopped for a coffee and chatted with my friends from the night before, Trevor and Leanne, during which time we were approached by a Canadian man called Damian, who remarked on the GoPro camera strapped to my chest as he invited himself to join us. At well over 6 feet tall, he was a physically intimidating fellow but full of warmth and humour that made him impossible to dislike. As we all got to know each other, Damian told us that he was racing to Santiago as fast as he could in order to get back in time for the running of the bulls in Pamplona a few weeks later. This is an event where a section of the streets is closed off to release a small group of bulls that will then chase after anyone mad enough to jump in amongst them. It takes place during the festival of San Fermín in honour of the third-century martyr and patron saint of Pamplona of the same name. After a couple of coffees, I was eager to hit the road, and so said my goodbyes to Trevor, Leanne and Damian, as I left our enclave for the ever-thinning Pyrenean air.

With no let-up in the climb, by the time I got to the top of the Pyrenees, the shoulder pain I was experiencing from the constant bouncing of my backpack had graduated from irritating to agonising. Each step forward felt like being on the business end of a thousand judo chops, which dominated my focus. Facing down and leaning forward, I didn't even notice that I, at some point, had crossed the border from France into Spain — not that I even cared at that moment as foremost in my mind was collapsing into the first bed I laid my eyes on. To make matters worse, I had forgotten entirely which route Nora had advised me to take down the mountain. I opted for the slightly shorter but more difficult passage to Roncesvalles, wincing my way through the majestic beech forest to my next stopping point. When I reached the literal fork in the road, my choices were between a direct, sharp descent through the woods and a meandering, gentle highway around it.

Roncesvalles was a name new to my ears, and I was interested to learn that the village holds an important place in not only French and Spanish history but also wider Europe — in particular, the Battle of Roncesvalles, which took place on the 25th of July 1813 between Anglo-Portuguese forces led by Major-General Galbraith Cole during the Peninsular War of 1808-1814. After the Duke of Wellington, Arthur

Wellesley's comprehensive victory over Joseph Bonaparte (older brother of Napoleon) at the battle of Vitoria, his forces pressed on in an attempt to capture the last remaining French strongholds of San Sebastian and Pamplona. Wellington split his forces and diverted 11,000 troops to blockade Pamplona, with a much smaller force sent to prevent any French counter-attack over the Pyrenees. French troops under General Reille based at Saint-Jean-Pied-de-Port advanced over the pass in an attempt to meet the 40,000 soldiers at Roncesvalles but were held back by the much smaller British force for several hours before finally forcing their retreat towards Pamplona. After reinforcements arrived, allied forces were able to make a stand at the battle of Sorauren, eventually forcing the French to retreat with heavy casualties on the 30th of July. Ultimately, Wellington would successfully capture both San Sebastian and Pamplona, eventually leading to the invasion of France.

When I eventually reached civilization, I came across the first of many STOP signs throughout the Camino that had been vandalised to read "Don't STOP Walking", which ironically was all I wanted to do. Gently sobbing, I steeled myself and trudged on with slumped shoulders across the world largest car park towards what seemed to be the only hotel in town, somehow missing the enormous sign for the cheap, well-appointed pilgrim hostel. Learning the nightly rate to be a hefty €50 was hastily followed by my teary-eyed agreement, while my shoulders, back and wallet cried out in pain, looking up at the gleaming face of Martin Sheen in picture form, taken during the filming of his movie, *The Way*. After a heavy bout of self-pity interspersed liberally with coarse language, I had a bath, which helped immensely with both. Since a three-course meal was included in my hotel fee, I bungled my way to the dining room at about 6 for a main course of fish. A whole one. Head, bones and everything. As I ate and drank wine, I chatted idly with a French man sitting beside me who was travelling The Way by bike — at least that is what I gathered from my limited French and his non-existent English. After dinner, I went to explore the small village centre, making sure to visit the fantastic, cheap pilgrim hostel I was missing out on, before bumping into the Scots having a drink, followed by a pilgrim mass at 8, during which several pilgrims were invited up to the altar to receive a blessing. While there, I sat next to a British man named Dave, who fidgeted throughout as if preoccupied. Whatever was bothering him, I was keen to help him with it since his constant glances into my eyeline were very much getting on my nerves. However, all was soon revealed when the time came for mass celebrants to give each other the sign of peace. To the uninitiated, there is a point during a catholic mass where worshippers are invited to offer each other the sign of peace by shaking hands with those around them and, since this custom only lasts for around 10 seconds, it usually only involves greeting those in your immediate vicinity. David, however, decided to attempt to break the world record for the fastest time for someone to get from one side of a packed church to the other. Before I could react, David was shuffling awkwardly down the pew, the back of his head mere inches from other bemused celebrants. Ignoring outstretched hands left and right as he went, he eventually made it to the other side, after which it became apparent that he was using this opportunity as an ice breaker to make the acquaintance of a young German girl he was clearly taken with. This episode didn't go unnoticed by several others, probably because I pointed it out loudly. I never saw either of them again after that day, so I have no idea if his advances got him anywhere, but I like to think that they did.

After mass, many of us went back to the bar, where I spent some time getting to know a father and son who were walking the Camino for a week before heading home. Father Kevin had travelled from Ireland with his youngest son Michael, aged 14, and planned to walk the whole Camino in four stages, one stage each year with each of his four children. While admirable, it was all or nothing in my case — I was going to walk the whole Camino or none of it. The idea of walking some, going home, then coming back to finish was out of the question. However, Kevin's explanation that walking the Camino was a way to bond with his children has become more relatable to me years later since becoming a father myself. Neither he nor Michael spoke very much on the occasions we were all in each other's company, but maybe walking in silence was the quality time this father and son might otherwise try to find in a more clichéd activity like fishing. After a few drinks, I was too tired to do anything else (not that there was anything else to do), so I returned to the hotel, ready to do it all again tomorrow. And the day after. And the day after that. Then I remembered that I still needed to wash and dry my sweat-sodden clothes that were currently festering in my hotel room corner. I hand-washed them in the tiny bathroom sink with minimal effort before hanging them up on my travel washing line that needed to be tied around the door and the shower rail for it to be capable of supporting the weight of saturated hiking gear. At 11pm, I finally clambered into bed and fell asleep to the sound of it falling down.

7

MIND YOUR LANGUAGE

||||||||||||||||||||||||||||||||||||||||||||||||||||||||||||||||||||||||||||||||||||||||||||||||||||||||||||||||||||||||||||||||||

I AWOKE AT 6 the next morning to a sensation that I could only describe as a hangover in my shoulders. With zero composure, a volley of swear words gave me enough adrenaline to rise from the bed, after which I lurched around robotically as I tried to keep my top half completely rigid. Dismayed at my earlier self for not making better preparations to leave that morning, I knew that a good breakfast was a must since I had to walk over 20km today. In what I am sure would have been a pitiful sight, I pulled my still-wet clothes up off the floor and put them on at glacial speed while praying to any deity to make me feel better because, after wrestling my 10kg backpack onto my back, I doubted I could feel any worse. I shuffled downstairs into the restaurant and choked down a stale croissant that was front and centre amongst the colourful yet unappetising breakfast bar. Despite the pain in my shoulders, I remained standing throughout, doubtful in my own ability to rise from a seated position.

As I left the hotel amongst a steady stream of pilgrims, I was met by the parish priest at the famous 790km to Santiago sign at the Roncesvalles town limits. He must have woken up at an ungodly hour to be out in time to wish each pilgrim a safe trip as they left his parish and, while I appreciated him taking the time to wish us a safe trip, 790 was still an incredibly disheartening number to see after a challenging first day. Meandering through the Pyrenees meant I had been walking a long way without getting very far as the crow flies. Although not at that moment, I would come to appreciate that first, tough day as the shock to the mind and body would serve me well for future days.

After about three hours of pleasant woodland scenery, I caught sight of a small elderly pilgrim sitting by the side of the path ahead of me. Deciding to leave him to take a break in peace, I walked straight past him, only to be called out to by name.

"Duncan?" he said.

I turned, recognising the man. It was Derek, the priest from Dundee.

"Derek!" I exclaimed, surprised at how glad I was to see a familiar face.

"Have you given up?" I asked.

Derek chuckled mightily before giving me a somewhat more detailed account of his day so far than I had expected, with something I would learn to be a daily ritual of his. He was up at 5 to say mass in his room (yes, you can do it alone apparently) before showering, followed by a light breakfast — ready to set off before anyone else. His approach was more hare than tortoise, as he explained that he anticipated that his inevitable rest would give familiar faces a chance to catch up — something he seemed delighted to see pay off.

Now, this is an abridged version of Derek's day — it took around 5 minutes of standing before him for me to give up and drop down beside the man. I was tired enough as it was, and there was no way I was doing an optional bonus round of standing in place. I was glad I did so and was fascinated to gain an insight into the day-to-day life of a priest as, despite being a Catholic growing up, I have never had significant interactions with priests outside of a church setting. After around 20 minutes of getting to know each other, we decided to set about attacking the last 8km of the stage to our overnight stop of Zubiri together. I stood up and became acquainted with another enemy of the pilgrim — something I un-affectionately dubbed, The Second Start. In my opinion, as difficult as starting to walk each day on the Camino was, resuming a walk after a rest was just as bad. My body seemed to be having some kind of allergic reaction to the resumption as if it were rebelling for being lied to. Insubordination from my own flesh wasn't going to stand and, therefore, future breaks would have to be kept to a minimum.

After finally settling into a steady pace, Derek and I enjoyed the last few kilometres as we entered the beautiful village of Zubiri. As you enter the village, you cross a quaint little bridge over the gently flowing Arga river, in which I couldn't resist cooling my aching feet alongside the other pilgrims already doing the same. At the same time, Derek took the opportunity to wash various items of walking gear in the water. On the bank of the river were dozens of the kind of flat, round stones that are perfect for skipping across water, so after the laundry, I decided to partake in the activity as I ate a few of the biscuits I had bought in St Jean on the first day. That was until I put a stone in my mouth and threw a biscuit. People saw.

As we ambled along the main street in Zubiri, Derek informed me that the municipal hostel would be where he would lay his head that night. In an experience I would rather not repeat, I had stayed in a youth hostel only once before, in Miami, Florida, when I was a student. On that occasion, I shared a small room with approximately forty thousand Australians, of which more than one brought "company" back with them while the rest of us desperately pretended to sleep. After voicing my misgivings, which were countered stubbornly with Derek's insistence, I yielded, and we sought out the albergue to find it a great deal less well-equipped when compared to the one in Roncesvalles. Off-white linens atop unhappy metal bed frames stretched out as far as the eye could see, bearing more than a passing resemblance to a first world war convalescent home — only here we had to remove our shoes upon entering. This, I presumed, to be a brand new policy judging by the ghastly state of the floor. Playing "The Floor Is Lava" with both myself and my possessions proved more difficult than I expected, and I was resigned to eventually putting all my clothes in a small pile on the floor while I made a meal of organising everything else. After handing over our pilgrim passports for validation, we settled into our modest surroundings, at which point I followed my soon-to-be standard routine of showering and getting my gear ready for the next day before foraging for food with Derek.

On the topic of food, I wasn't terribly worried about the types I might encounter on the Camino. Years of being too embarrassed to say anything if I didn't like the look of what was served to me when having dinner at school friends' houses had forced me to try new foods, giving me the habit of seeking out items on a menu I had never eaten, however unusual. The first restaurant we entered was on the opposite side of town and was completely devoid of staff and customers, which made us initially think it was closed. As we turned to leave, a moustached gentleman appeared from the back, wiping his hands on his apron, leaving a dark red stain. I gulped, but before words could escape my mouth, broken Italian began leaving Derek's. I can only assume that either he mistook what country we were in or believed Italian and Spanish to be similar enough to be understood by speakers of either. The furrowed brow of our host caused me to suspect that this wasn't the case, and his angry gesticulations towards the menu overhead confirmed it.

Derek opened his mouth to change feet.

"Grazie", he muttered, although what he was actually thanking the staff member for remains a mystery. Preferring to avoid having my food spat into, I motioned to Derek that it was time to leave, possibly giving our new friend the impression that Derek was an escaped nursing home resident and I, his incompetent carer. We hastily headed back to the main intersection and set up camp at an outside table of the bustling, Taberna Baserri, eventually settling for the incredibly popular and prominently advertised, 'El menu Pellegrino' or 'Pilgrim Menu', where we were joined shortly afterwards by Trevor and Leanne. The pilgrim's menu is available at restaurants throughout the Camino route and usually consists of a three-course meal and a drink for only €10 — this was providing you were a pilgrim, although no proof was demanded of us. The set meal would prove to be a mainstay throughout my Camino and was welcome sustenance to someone frequently out of his head with hunger and, since food was the second biggest outgoing in terms of expenses, it was as welcome to the wallet as it was to the stomach. During the meal, Derek joked about walking to the church nearby adjacent to the restaurant, helping himself to robes and saying mass as the topic of conversation turned to what we all did for a living. We all took a short stroll together around the village centre when I noticed Trevor had a pronounced limp from that day's hike. Not wanting to aggravate any potential injury, he and Leanne decided to take a taxi to the next town, where they would be staying in slightly loftier accommodation than the municipal albergue, giving Trevor a chance to get off his feet.

Meanwhile, I decided to shatter my record of consecutive days where I attended mass and go for a second day in a row, where I arrived to see that Derek hadn't been joking. There he was, standing at the altar in ill-fitting robe, celebrating mass alongside his Spanish counterpart — each of them without a word of the other's language in their heads. From a lay person's perspective, I thought it went relatively smoothly, and I left mass in an improved mood to phone my wife. After a quick chat about the day I had, I retired to my luxurious foam pad at the albergue, where I found that Derek had somehow not only managed to get there before me but had time to change into his pyjamas and fall fast asleep. I lay down in the clothes I had on, ready for Pamplona, the first big city of my Camino so far.

8

LOST OR STOLEN

IIIIIIIIIIIIIIIIIIIIIIIIIIIIIIIIIIIIIIIIIIIIIIIIIIIIIIIIIIIIIIIIIIIIIIIIIIIIIIIIIIIIIIIIIII

"ASK NOT FOR whom the bell tolls!" Derek exclaimed as the church bell rang out during breakfast the following day, in reference to our impending arrival in Pamplona later that day. *For Whom the Bell Tolls* is the title of the Ernest Hemingway novel published in 1940, and Hemingway himself is credited in no small part with helping put Pamplona on the map. Shortly after reaching the city proper, you will see a bust of him residing outside the Plaza de Toros de Pamplona — the third largest bullring in the world. To be honest, my knowledge of Hemingway's connection to Pamplona was fleeting at best, but outside the bullring is probably the most appropriate place for it due to his reputation for being 'bullish' in nature. As an aside, I am not in favour of bullfighting, nor am I vehemently against it. I consider it to be at best poor form and at worst condescending to appropriate one's own ethics on those of another culture, so I keep my nose well and truly out of it. After hearing a couple of Spanish colleagues, polar opposite in opinion on the subject, having a full-on shouting match in the middle of the office has caused me to forever swerve the topic in a public forum.

American writer Ernest Miller Hemingway is famous across the world and is closely associated with several places in it — Florida, Cuba and Paris, to name but a few, but before all of these came Pamplona. Even in 2014, Pamplona hardly seemed enormous to my eyes, but the handful of trips Hemingway made to the capital of Navarre between 1923 and 1927 were less to a city than they were to an insignificant, sun-baked outpost. The young writer was drawn to Pamplona by the San Fermin festival — famed for its running of the bulls, even today. Now the location of the statue definitely made sense. Hemingway's first (and some say finest) novel, *The Sun Also Rises*, was published in the middle of these Spanish years in 1926, in which he waxed lyrical about the San Fermin festival, opening Pamplona to the world of the 'roaring twenties' in the process, and was loosely based on Hemingway's own hedonistic experiences of Spanish summers. If you go to the Café Iruña on the Plaza del Castillo, you can meet the man himself, albeit in statue form. With enormous mirrors under the elaborate ceiling, the cafe itself seems to be a time capsule for when Hemingway and Pamplona were most in love. Somewhat paradoxically, the statue depicts the man as a more recognisable, much older version of himself, when this was certainly not the case when his flesh and blood walked the streets of Pamplona. As he stands in the former smoking section of the cafe, his frustrated expression adequately conveys how he probably would have regarded the indoor smoking ban introduced in 2011.

It would be no exaggeration to say that Hemingway eventually fell out of love with Pamplona. His final visit was in 1959, where his ageing mind and body were met by an equally tired city under the grip of fascism under General Franco. How strange it must have been for Hemingway that his books were now banned in the very place that inspired his first. He observed, in *The Dangerous Summer*, not published until 1985, 24 years after his death, that Pamplona was "as it always was, except forty thousand tourists have been added".

On the morning of the 2nd of July 1961, just two years after writing those words, Hemingway walked onto his porch at his home in Ketchum, Idaho, put his shotgun in his mouth, and pulled the trigger. While it is no doubt that Hemingway had his demons — his father had taken his own life years before — one cannot help to notice the morbid coincidence that Hemingway left this world during the week of San Fermin. Now, in no way am I suggesting that his suicide was intended to coincide with the festival, but the mutation of his beloved Pamplona did make Hemingway unhappy — as did many other things. I entered Pamplona myself that day with a sense of curious irony that I was part of what Hemingway came to dislike about the place he both raised and ruined. Unlike Hemingway, I was entering Pamplona several weeks before San Fermin and was therefore still able to get an affordable hotel room (something as rare as hen's teeth during the festival), to find heaving with people as it was. As I reached Pamplona's crowded town centre, the tall buildings and narrow, pedestrianised streets were a welcome respite from the baking Spanish sun.

Hemingway's references to the Camino itself are fleeting, and there is no record of him actually walking any part of The Way. That said, I would probably be naive in thinking that the Spanish musician from Chapter 1 was the only famous person to have walked it, so I decided to research who I may have run into had I walked the Camino at another time, or even lifetime. Several prominent figures have travelled the way down the years, from royalty to writers. A fact I would later learn was that just a month after I completed my Camino, German chancellor, Angela Merkel walked a section of the Way with her Spanish opposite number, Mariano Rajoy, in what was viewed as a significant show of solidarity from Germany to Spain during the latter's difficult economic recovery.

Not every famous pilgrim can be accused of using the Camino to curry political favour. In all honesty, there is no way of knowing a person's real reason for undertaking this walk, whether it be spiritual in nature or not. Possibly the earliest 'celebrity' to walk the Camino de Santiago was a French monk named Aymeric Picaud. His account of his journey around 1140 AD can be found in the fifth book of the 'Codex Calixtinus', considered to be the world's first tourist guide. More recently, Martin Sheen, directed by his son, Emilio Estevez, had first-hand experience of the Camino while shooting a movie about the pilgrimage in 2010. Sheen's own father was born just outside Santiago, and he was already familiar with the Camino, hoping to even walk it one day. While on a break from filming The West Wing in 2003, Sheen travelled part of the Way by car with his grandson, Taylor, who met his future wife while she was waiting tables at a restaurant they visited. After explaining to his son why he left his grandson somewhere in northern Spain, the story eventually developed into his project 6 years later.

Sheen was not the first actor drawn to the Way by a project. In 1994, actress Shirley MacLaine walked the French route amid a personal crisis, walking up to 20km a day at the age of 60. She stayed at hostels, visited churches, and could reasonably be considered to have had a genuine pilgrim experience. She even wrote a book detailing her spiritual and physical take on The Way: *The Camino: A Journey of the Spirit*. Another actor, two-time Academy Award winner Anthony Quinn, starred in a miniseries in 1999 named after the Camino and made the most to learn about the route while filming. In 1987, Brazilian novelist Paulo Coelho released a book chronicling his experiences while walking the Camino Frances the previous year, later the inspiration for his 1988 bestseller *The Alchemist*. Many of his books can be traced back to various points along the Way, and Coelho is often credited with helping revive the Camino as a tourist attraction due to the marked increase in pilgrim numbers after the release of his seminal novel. Actor-cum-travel writer Andrew McCarthy walked the Camino in 2012 and was inspired to include his experience in his debut book, *The Longest Way Home*, which chronicled various journeys he took around the world, thus launching his second career as a prolific travel writer. And finally, a reminder to let no level of disability be an excuse, British physicist Stephen Hawking completed a section of the Way in Galicia in 2008.

I had awoken that morning to another day of glorious Spanish sunshine. I embarked on the most leisurely day of walking so far and, for the first time, felt like I was getting into a groove at this walking lark. As I walked, I got talking to a pilgrim from Cordoba named Pablo, who immediately stood out because of his walking companion — a gorgeous black labrador called Mimi. The dog was so well trained, she didn't need to be on a lead as she remained glued to her master's side, only breaking her focus on the road ahead to briefly gaze at him in exaltation. After an hour or so walking, I stopped to share brunch with Pablo, Mimi and some loitering chickens, where the human told me about his intention to walk the entire Camino with his beloved dog over the next three months, averaging around 10km a day — something he assured me was not too much for her. After wishing them well, I ploughed on and managed to reach the vibrant metropolis of Pamplona in a respectable 5 hours.

Any semblance of a good mood soon evaporated after a frustrating walk around Pamplona's city centre. I eventually gave up trying to find the municipal hostel (or any hostel for that matter), settling instead for a hotel — which was at least still reasonably priced considering we were still a couple of weeks from the San Fermin festival. During that time, hotel rates have been known to double or even triple. Although I wasn't financially in a position to stay in a hotel every night, there is something to be said about not sleeping more than a few inches from somebody else, not to mention the opportunity to wash and dry my clothes as well as myself more comfortably. After performing said tasks, I decided it was high time for some day-drinking, and that day's pilgrim menu at the first bar I happened across did not disappoint. When the waiter brought out a bottle of red wine, I assumed that I would be charged for what I took and limited myself to around a third throughout the three courses. To my confusion, the bill he brought out to me once I had finished came to a total of €10. My furrowed brow caught the attention of a young man sitting a few tables away, who couldn't help but ask what had me so bewildered. Over the next few minutes, he explained to me in excellent English how a bottle of wine is included in most set menus in Pamplona. As someone who has spent his entire drinking career being used to it costing around £5 for but a glass, this came as a pleasant surprise. Since I had most of this one left, I offered it to him, but he politely declined as he was late for his shift. At the very bar we were sitting outside of. After polishing it off and feeling suitably inebriated, I took a bottle of water with me to try and sober up, which was more expensive than the wine. I wondered what comes out of the taps in Pamplona.

From there, I walked over to the well-staffed, bilingual tourist office for recommendations on what one should see when spending an afternoon in Pamplona, where I was delighted to see that they had their own stamp for pilgrims. I took my passport out and placed it on the counter, only to notice that I hadn't — before me on the counter were the credentials of one Father Derek Geraghty. In a wholly disproportionate fit of panic, I envisioned myself being denied my Compostela in Santiago a few weeks in the future because I appeared to have walked the Camino pretending to be somebody else. Immediately, I about-turned and left the office. Out of desperation, I began to walk (actually, the ever-growing blisters on my feet made it more of an ungainly hobble) around the centre of Pamplona like a lost dog in search of his master. This was made doubly burdonsome by the throng of people filling the streets to watch that night's opening match of the 2014 World Cup. I found it disconcerting enough to find my bearings in sparsely populated towns and villages of the Camino, but in this bustling city-centre, it was a great deal more arduous, and the number of people surrounding me seemed to be mounting now that I needed to find one in particular. I knew Derek had a nose for finding out the municipal hostel like a bargain-hunting bloodhound and thought he would probably have a better chance than I of succeeding. It actually turned out there were three municipal hostels in Pamplona, all relatively close to one another. After fruitless searches at the first two, I was hoping for the best but fearing the worst. When I arrived at the last municipal hostel, I asked the young man at the reception if he had a record of Derek staying there. His limited English made it clear to me that he couldn't just give out guest information, but what he could do, was leave the tannoy microphone alone while he left the room. Reading between the lines, I waited for him to leave my sight before taking the microphone, appealing for Derek to come forward. When no priest was forthcoming, I left the hostel dejected, admitting to myself that I couldn't be even sure that he even had my passport.

Downcast at losing a piece of folded cardboard I had only owned for three days, I lay on my hotel bed when an idea struck me. Since Derek was a priest, he would likely be a prominent figure in his local community, meaning there must be a chance, however slight, that he has some kind of online presence. Common social media platforms yielded nothing, but lo and behold, after a few minutes of grasping at straws, a phone number for a Fr. Derek Geraghty was on the screen before me. Even in the best-case scenario, all I expected was to have the chance to speak to someone back in Scotland who could advise me on the best way to reach the wandering cleric. To my utter amazement, I got through to the man himself. It's a small world made even smaller when you open your mouth.

It turned out that Derek had anticipated the mass (pardon the pun) of people there would be in Pamplona and stayed a few kilometres back on the trail to avoid it. He promised to meet me bright and early the next morning in the town square so we could return our passports to their rightful owners. Out of relief, I found myself gushing over the phone at the poor man like I was his biggest fan upon hearing his words. To be honest, at that moment, I probably was. Relieved, I lay on the bed and enjoyed the opening match of the 2014 World cup between Brazil and Croatia, ready to meet my new hero in the morning. I stretched out on the bed, keen to savour what would probably be the more comfortable end of the spectrum in terms of accommodation. Going back to the more rustic options along the Way from the relative luxury of a town like Pamplona was not a welcome thought. However, I suspect it makes for a more interesting story.

9

FOOTLOOSE

|||||||||||||||||||||||||||||||||||||||||||||||||||||||||||||||

THE BRIGHT AND sunny Pamplona morning found me in the small town square adjacent to the tourist office, where I eagerly awaited Derek's arrival. To me, the tourist office was an obvious choice for a rendezvous point as it was a piece of cake for us both to find, as well as being conveniently located on the Camino route itself, which was lined through the town with brass seashells either side of the thoroughfare. Before long, Derek was beside me to share a laugh at the situation as if we were old friends as we swapped credentials. Across the square, I noticed two policemen were watching our exchange with some interest, although not enough to approach us. After surveying the scene, I suspect that they were content that no drug dealers would be so stupid to perform a transaction at such a time and place. After a few more minutes chatting about our respective adventures the previous day, Derek and I made the unfamiliar journey of actually setting off together, rather than me playing catch-up. We made our way out of town through some parks and past the university before reaching the suburbs, where we stopped for a break in the quaint village of Cizur Menor. It was here we became acquainted with two Australian pilgrims on their fourth Camino who helpfully warned us that if we were planning on spending the night in the next village of Zariquiegui, then we should feed ourselves at a cafe or bring supplies with us as, in the village, we would find neither. Since we had technically already started climbing the mountain of Alto de Perdon, Derek and I were confident we had it in us to push on a bit further, so Puerta La Reina was recommended. Grateful to our new friends, off we set.

At around 800 metres at its peak, Alto de Perdon can barely be considered a mountain and, although strenuous enough, neither Derek nor I were out of breath at any point as we scaled up to the summit. After around half an hour of silent walking, Derek gave me a fright when he suddenly and very loudly pointed at an old stone fountain in the centre of a semicircular stone wall. This, according to his research, was the legendary Fuente Reniega or Fountain of Denial. He went on to relay to me the story of a pilgrim, weary and thirsty from climbing the mountain, who was tempted by the devil to renounce God in exchange for life-saving water. When the pilgrim refused, the devil again offered to quench his thirst if he rejected the Virgin Mary. Again, the young man refused. Eager to make a deal, Satan asked for the pilgrim to only deny Saint James the Apostle. When the pilgrim chose to die of thirst over this, he cried out to the heavens, and the devil was gone. Upon opening his eyes, the pilgrim saw Saint James himself stood before him, and made the fountain appear, rewarding his faith. While hardly a convincing story, I maintain that the least credible thing about it was that Derek had done some research. A few hours later, we reached the summit of Alto del Perdon to find it topped with metallic Camino themed sculptures created by Vincente Galbete, collectively known as the *Monument to the Pilgrim's Way*. Derek and I removed our backpacks to loosen up, spending a few minutes taking in the spectacular vistas. I was ready to continue on to Puerta La Reina, but

Derek was going to stay awhile longer to put aloe vera on his heavily sunburnt calves, assuring that he would catch up with me later.

Coming down the mountain was far less enjoyable than going up it. Plenty of gravel and loose rocks underfoot made it incredibly easy to slip or roll one's ankle (judging by the fact I was able to expertly demonstrate both) but, mercifully, by the time you pass through the medieval towns of Uterga and Muruzabal, the slope eases significantly. About 2km before reaching Puerta La Reina is the town of Obanos. Here, Guillermo, Duke of Aquitaine, is said to have stayed while returning home after making a pilgrimage to Santiago with his sister, Felicia. It is believed that he killed her when Felicia did not want to return to the French court with him. Guilt-ridden, the duke returned to Santiago to pray for forgiveness before returning to Obanos, where he stayed as penance for the rest of his life. Facts are difficult to nail down about the story, but a play called *The Mystery of Obanos* is performed in the town square on alternate years to fill in the blanks using between three and four hundred Obanos townsfolk as extras. I would definitely have bought a ticket to watch but, unfortunately, it was about a month too early. About half an hour after leaving Obanos, I reached the point where the Camino Frances and the Camino Aragonese meet and my next resting point, Puente La Reina.

Known locally as the Puente Romanico, Puente La Reina is famed for its Romanesque bridge over the Arga River. The town itself literally translates into English as "Bridge of the Queen", named as such in honour of Queen Muniadona, wife of King Sancho III, who built the six-arched bridge in the 11th century, to help pilgrims such as myself on their way to Santiago. A small chapel once stood in the middle of the bridge, atop of which a statue of Our Lady of the Puy, the patron saint of Estella, could be found. Local folklore tells the story of how a small bird would sometimes clean the statue's face, signalling good omens. Although the chapel is now gone, the statue itself was moved to the

Church of San Pedro Apostol in the Basque capital of Vitoria-Gasteiz in the 19th century. The town itself was founded in 1122 and was owned by the Knights Templar until their expulsion from Spain in 1312.

Auspiciously, you are almost guided straight into an albergue immediately after entering Puente La Reina before crossing the most famous bridge on the Camino Frances. I was grateful to have been denied an opportunity to get lost and before I knew it, was flinging my backpack down on the lower bunk of the private hostel located just inside the town limits. As I did so, a familiar voice behind me called out, "Hey, GoPro dude!"

It was Damian, the Canadian prison guard I had met on my first day of walking. Remember how I said his goal to get to Santiago and back in time for the running of the bulls was ambitious? Well, here is how it went down, or rather, came up. For you see, Damian had been making questionable choices when it came to dining to save time. For instance, he would buy all of his meals in the evening after a full day of walking to have them packed for the next day, allowing him to eat on the move, thus covering more ground with the outcome of a quicker Camino. It transpired that the stuffy conditions of a non-air conditioned municipal hostel at the height of a Spanish summer were not a stellar example of food hygiene, resulting in a hefty dose of food poisoning for poor Damian by the time he reached Pamplona. Now, sickness didn't just slow him down, it completely took him out of commission for two days, during which he spent plenty of quality time with his hotel room toilet, into which several rounds of stomach/bowel contents were emptied. The time off the trail was enough for Damian to realise that there was no way he was going to make it back to Pamplona in time for San Fermin, and so he had resolved to enjoy his Camino at a more leisurely pace.

Truthfully, I wasn't faring too well myself physically. Shoulder and back pain had been replaced in my ruminating by sizable blisters on my feet that were becoming painful enough for Damian to notice my altered gait. He told me about Tom, an American doctor he had met that morning, who was helping pilgrims with the exact problem I was having. It just so happened that Tom was a few bunk beds down from us, so I decided to go and see him. I rather sheepishly introduced myself to him, expecting him to justifiably be annoyed at me for disturbing him from a post-hike snooze, but my misgivings were completely unfounded as meeting Tom was a fantastic experience. This was not only because he increased my comfort levels exponentially by draining all of my disgusting blisters but also because of the genuine care he exuded towards fellow pilgrims such as myself. Tom was doing the Camino with his wife (a nurse) and two children for the third time, going out of his way to help his fellow walkers, something for which I had tremendous respect. If two kids under the age of 12 can hike all day without complaining, I could too. If, in the unlikely event you are unable to locate an American doctor to personally drain blisters for you by hand, there are dozens of Pharmacies along the route that are well experienced at taking care of whatever revolting ailments a pilgrim might throw at one.

On that note, I must say that the pharmacies in Spain were a tremendous credit to the country. Taking Tom's advice, later that day, I decided to purchase some of the supplies he suggested to prevent the blisters from reappearing. There was only one pharmacy in Puente La Reina, but within seconds of stepping through the door, the English speaking pharmacist came out from behind the counter to approach me as I stood confused before the plasters. As she approached wearing a friendly smile, I immediately felt at ease, assuming she had anticipated my problem and was shortly about to solve it.

"Hello." She soothed, "You are looking for condoms?"

Perhaps I am misremembering an inflexion at the end of her statement, retrospectively clinging to the hope that it was a question rather than a directive. As I stammered in response, I wordlessly lifted up my foot to show her the cluster of drained blisters on the outside of my little toe, significantly failing to either correct her on the condom reference or recognise that she was speaking English, rendering gesticulations unnecessary. Thankfully I was quickly able to compose myself and make it clear that I did not mistake my blisters for a sexually transmitted disease but simply sought the typical treatment of plasters for them.

Later that evening, I took advantage of the nightly football, bumping into Trevor and Leanne in the local bar where we watched the Netherlands trounce our host nation 5–1 where, strangely, the loudest celebrations in the bar came from the locals. I was somewhat taken aback at the volume of anti-Spanish sentiment throughout the Camino, particularly in the Basque region. I gathered from the distinct lack of Spanish flags (in place of which was what I later learned to be the Basque flag known as the Ikurriña) that the people in that region are fiercely protective of their cultural identity. After being accepted to the Spanish constitution in 1978 despite fierce opposition to the region's population, many still fail to identify with Madrid at all. Anti-Spanish graffiti seemed to be everywhere I looked, and I was unsure whether the imminent coronation of King Felipe VI had stirred up this level of vitriol in the graffiti artists of the Basque country or if it was always this strong. It was news to me that Basque is one of the five official languages in Spain (along with Catalan, Aranese, Galician, and Castilian) and, if you look carefully, you will notice different names for the same places in that region. For instance, Roncesvalles, the town I had not long left, would be known locally in Basque as Orreaga. The difference is most likely due to the Basque language being the last remaining descendant of pre-indo European languages in Western Europe, made all the more remarkable since it is entirely surrounded by the Latin-based variety. After a few drinks and a few laughs, I laid down, satisfied with that day's efforts. That was until I remembered I had left my phone charger at the hotel in Pamplona. Jesus wept.

10

A FOOL AND HIS MONEY

||||||||||||||||||||||||||||||||||||||||||||||||||||||||||||||||||||||||||||||||||||||||||||||||||||||||||||

HITTING THE ROAD at 6.30 every day almost always guarantees you to be the first to leave the hostel, with the majority of the other pilgrims barely stirring at such an hour. Despite the collective effort of all my roommates to make the most noise possible while sleeping, I still tried to make my way out as quietly as possible each time I left in the morning. The feeling that I was living the same day over and over again was already becoming tiresome.

Observe.

0600: Wake up to eat breakfast

0615: Get up but don't eat breakfast

0630: Start walking

1330: Stop walking

1430: Eat junk

1500: Wash/dry clothes

1600: Make inadequate preparations for the next day

1700: Explore my surroundings/get drunk

2200: Bedtime

2300: Actually go to bed

Behind schedule, I set off from the hostel at around 7, crossing the bridge to leave Puente la Reina from the opposite side I came in from. I was pessimistic about how the day might pan out when I encountered a pretty steep climb so soon after leaving the village, but the gradient eventually evened out much to my relief. As the trail straddled the N11 highway rather closely, I was concerned that the Camino was going to be along roads and motorways much more often as my pilgrimage progressed but, in due course, car engines and tarmac gave way to wildlife and farmland in what was a lively mix of both. The villages of Mañeru and Cirauqui were welcome breaks, if not for stopping for a coffee then for something else to look at other than the road ahead. The Roman road as you leave the latter is lined with pencil-like cypress trees that guide you over the Roman bridge in the direction of the Salado river, over which you cross to get to the municipality of Lorca. Not that I was minded to drink it (even if I was thirsty), it is said by none other than Picaud himself that the water of the Salado is deadly to both man and beast, stating:

Take care not to drink the water here, neither yourself nor
your horse, for it is a deadly river! On the way to Santiago, we
came across two Navarrese sitting by the bank, sharpening
the knives they used to flay pilgrims' horses which had drunk
the water and died. We asked them if the water was fit to drink,
and they lyingly replied that it was, whereupon we gave it to
our horses to drink. Two of them dropped dead at once, and
the Navarrese flayed them there and then.

I looked around and was relieved to see no knife-wielding miscreants sharpening knives. Furthermore, if they had designs to flay my non-existent horse and I, then stealing those matching raincoats I nearly purchased would probably have satisfied them. Lorca came and went without significance, and I passed the ruins of Hospital de Peregrinos de Arandigoyen, built in 1066, before reaching Villatuerta. Although it was a slightly longer walk, the markedly lower temperature that day made it infinitely more enjoyable. The fact that it was Saturday also allowed me to take more pleasure in this day's hike before my planned rest day tomorrow. However, the further I walked that day, the more I contemplated that doing so would be taking a rest day simply for the sake of it, which didn't seem to be an acceptable reason anymore. I was hitting my stride in terms of my routine, the unsightly blisters were all but gone, and there was no pain to speak of anywhere on my body for the first time since I set off from St Jean. I fancied I had now broken the back of it and was ready to go every day until I reached Santiago and, while physically the first week was tough, others had it worse than I. Just after passing the town of Villatuerta, I overtook a man who was walking barefoot for reasons I can only hypothesize. I winced with each pained step I witnessed, making my few blisters pale in comparison. Thereafter, I began silently ranking levels of suffering in my fellow pilgrims, for which he was to be the benchmark, a competition of which only I was to be aware and for which I regarded myself to be qualified. Anyone with an Irish mother knows how good they are at one-upping anyone when it comes to hardship. Should I ever complain about the walk to school, she relayed how she walked further. In the rain. Or the snow. Or barefoot in the snow. Or barefoot in the snow walking backwards because the wind was so fierce.

I was still in two minds on whether I was going to rest the next day, so I decided it prudent to find a hotel as opposed to a hostel where I would assuredly be limited to one night, although I did note the location of the municipal hostel just as you enter Estella's old town in case I decided to switch accommodation tomorrow. As it happened, Estella appeared to be an excellent place to spend a rest day, and some of its approximately 13,000 residents were enjoying the sun at some of its many cafes and restaurants in the main square of Plaza de los Fueros.

Founded in 1090, Estella was built on top of the former village of Lizarra and quickly thrived due to its location on the Camino Frances. This wealth is reflected in the stunning Romanesque architecture as the granting of a charter by King Sancho Ramirez encouraged French and Jewish merchants to settle here. When the local Navarrese were granted the same privileges as the established Jewish and French settlers in the 12th century, Estella eventually became divided into the three main areas of San Miguel, San Juan and San Pedro. These areas fought with each other often, with Jews, French and Navarrese living separately in each district. Europe's changeable sentiments towards the Jews would be reflected in the Navarrese civil war of 1451, during which the Jewish population in Estella was decimated. The situation would continue to vary wildly until the Jews were eventually expelled from Spain in 1492.

I was feeling pretty good and, since hotels are not subject to the fierce competition for beds that albergues are, decided to go straight to the tourist office in Plaza San Martin, just a stone's throw from the municipal hostel. Armed with a map of Estella, I was pleased to see that everything worth seeing was relatively close together for a town this size, starting with the Palace of the Kings, built in the 12th century and located right next door. Disused since the 15th century, the building became an art gallery and museum in 1991. From there, it was a two-minute walk to another 12th-century building, the church of San Pedro de la Rua. What is most interesting about this church is that it contained the remains of a 13th century Greek bishop. The Bishop of Patras died during his sleep while walking the Camino in disguise and was buried in the pilgrim cemetery. After the burial, witnesses claimed the pilgrim's grave glowed, resulting in the body being exhumed with his belongings being examined more closely. It turned out the man's walking stick was, in fact, a crozier, and amongst his possessions was a piece of the true cross and bone fragment belonging to Saint Andrew. It was only then that his actual identity was discovered.

Feeling tired yet content with my exploration, I found a cheap hotel adjacent to the main square and took a much-welcomed shower. Since it was still only mid-afternoon, I took the opportunity to do nothing but stretch out on my firm, single bed. I turned on the TV that looked old enough to be in a museum and, probably due to its advanced state of disrepair, only played one channel, on which a Spanish dubbed version of the Hugh Grant movie, *Nine Months*, was playing. I persevered for what felt like 9 months (but was actually about 30 seconds) before dozing off.

I awoke an hour later completely famished. There were no snacks left in my bag to tide me over, so I headed back the way I had come earlier into the main square to find a restaurant. Not for the first time, I found myself bewildered by the Spanish way of dining as there were so many identical-looking tables and chairs in the square, it was unclear which restaurant you were patronising when you sat at one. I saw Derek sitting on the opposite side with three other people and meandered my way over to join them. Derek introduced them to me as brothers-in-law, Jake and Peter from Aberdeen, and Bernard, an elderly German man residing in Chicago. I joined the others in ordering some tapas from a waitress (although from which restaurant I had no idea) as we all got to know each other a little better. I explained to the group that my mind was made to no longer take tomorrow as a rest day but to continue walking. Sadly, Derek had taken such a liking to our host town for the day, Estrella, that he would do the opposite by treating himself to an extra night in the hotel and would not leave town until Monday, making this the last day we would walk together. Derek's revelation didn't come as a total surprise since he was at best going to walk for two more days anyway, after which he was to head north by bus to Bilbao, from where he would fly home. It turned out that he had already checked into the same hotel I had, so we made a point of meeting the next morning for breakfast before our paths diverged.

Jake and Peter were unusual chaps. I recognised them in passing from previous days and, on each occasion, something about the pair stood out that I couldn't quite put my finger on. As we ate, drank and laughed together, it eventually dawned on me that, on precisely none of the occasions I had been in the same vicinity as them were either of them carrying bags. When I finally asked them about it, they educated me on the existence of specialist taxi companies in the region who, for a small fee, would take your bag to the next checkpoint, thus sparing you from carrying it. Such a service seemed to defeat the point of pilgrimage a bit, although the pair were unapologetic about any perceived corner-cutting and were walking the Camino to enjoy themselves entirely unencumbered by backpacks — and they were succeeding. Thoroughly indoctrinated, I knew that this was the choice for me. Instead of taking a rest day, I would treat myself to a twenty-mile walk instead of a slog. I took down the phone number from Jake and went back to the hotel to dial it. It was a struggle, but I managed to make enough sense to the man on the other end of the line to successfully book a bag collection for 9 o'clock the next morning. Jake had also given me the name of his hotel, the Hotel Yerri, which was in the tiny village of Sansol, 25km from Estella, which was essential as I would need a physical address to which my backpack could be delivered. All that was left to do was obtain one of the company's thousand or so envelopes scattered over the desk in my hotel's lobby, stuff €10 into it, and leave it with my bag. What could be simpler? Feeling revitalised, I went out for a few drinks with my fellow pilgrims, deciding to have a nice lie-in in the morning, unaware of the calamity soon to befall me.

11

FEAR AND LOATHING
IN LOS ARCOS

||||||||||||||||||||||||||||||||||||||||||||||||||||||||||||||||||||||||||||||||||||||||||||||||||||

IT TURNS OUT that a lie-in during the Camino for me meant rising from the bed at 6.30 instead of 6.15. I got dressed and made my way down to the nearby cafe to see Derek already there tucking into a vast plate of food. With virtually no appetite, I joined him and tried to ignore the mounting worry of soon being separated from my bag as he proceeded to eat his own breakfast, followed by most of mine. Despite the conversation with Derek being jovial, nothing could stop my thoughts from returning to the fate of my bag once it was out of my possession. I am generally not mistrusting, but this bag collection service still seemed a bit too good to be true and, for this reason, I decided that I would amble around town until I saw someone come to collect my bag with my own eyes. Breakfast over, Derek and I embraced, wishing each other a heartfelt "Buen Camino!" I hope they look after him in Italy.

I nursed my coffee for a few minutes before returning to the hotel, where I completed the collection envelope and left my bag by the front door of the building as instructed before checking out. I sat on a bench directly facing the other side of that front door of my hotel, with 9 o'clock coming and going during which my bag covered as much distance as I did. At around ten past, a gaunt-looking man wearing a flannel shirt marched up to the front door and stepped inside. While I had no idea if he was the bag collector, I wouldn't have been surprised if he owned a windowless van judging by the look of him. Sure that it must be him, even the half-hour of waiting for him to re-emerge wasn't going to convince me otherwise. Almost 45 minutes after entering, he finally surfaced with my bag slung over his shoulder, and since, by this time of the day, I would typically be halfway to the next stopping point, I really needed to get going to avoid being on the wrong side of a 'NO VACANCY' sign. Almost immediately, my decision to have the bag sent on felt like a masterstroke, yielding the first day since my journey started that I enjoyed the actual walking part. A combination of 10kg less on my back and switching to open-toed sandals felt like I was walking on air in comparison. As I left Estrella, I briefly passed some time talking to a British pilgrim, a man from Portsmouth named Martin, who had snuck up behind me before I could notice. At first, he seemed keen to speak, but my modest pace must have been an annoyance because it wasn't long before he power walked out of my sight and into my memory. This was for the best as I needed to pay close attention to my surroundings in order to find what is possibly the Camino's most peculiar feature.

As you leave the metropolitan area of Estrella and move into the suburbs, you will find the ancient Monastery of Irache in Ayegui, where you can discover the famous Fuente del Vino wine fountain. Built in 1991, the fountain is easy to miss since visiting it involves taking a slight detour away from the trail and many pilgrims look forward to doing so, hopefully due to its novelty rather than any alcohol dependency. That said, overlooking the fountain is a security camera accompanied by a contender for the most ignored sign in history:

We are pleased to invite you to drink in moderation. If you wish to take the wine with you, you will have to buy it.

Somewhat predictably, the camera and sign were promptly disregarded by the half-dozen or so people there already. I visited the adjoining water fountain first as I rather childishly thought it looked lonely in comparison. As I approached the wine fountain, two pilgrims from Seattle were happily filling up an empty 2-litre bottle with some of the hundreds of litres of red wine collected daily from the surrounding vineyards without a care in the world for what the baking heat was going to do to the wine's flavour profile. Sure enough, later that day, I had to politely decline their kind offer of '*getting on this*' as they gesticulated their half-drunk bottle of lukewarm wine at me, presumably after they had downed a heroic amount themselves. I earnestly tried a small amount using my plastic water bottle and was pleasantly surprised that it hadn't been warmed by the sweltering day we were having. I'm no sommelier, but I know what I hate, and I didn't hate this wine. It was bog standard table wine — no more, no less, and if it cost any more than free, I doubt any other soul but I would be interested.

Unfortunately, there was one arguably quirkier feature of the Camino that I could not experience. The village of Azqueta is where you can rejoin The Way and is home to a man known locally as Pablito, who provides homemade walking sticks to pilgrims. Doing so since he was a boy, Pablito is now well into his eighties and claims to have given away over 30,000 sticks in his lifetime, for which he refuses any payment. He wasn't there when I passed through, but as I did, I made a silent prediction to myself that I would see at least one pilgrim at the airport in Santiago try and take a wooden stick taller than themselves onto the aircraft as a personal item. Leaving Azqueta, I was heading uphill to the highest point of the day at Villamayor de Monjardín with still a couple of hours to go before reaching the next major town of Los Arcos, shortly beyond which was my designated stopping point of Sansol. Despite the sweltering temperatures, I was rather enjoying myself (not to mention making great time), so I decided to reward myself with a beer from a roadside cafe and a nice long rest. "This is going well!" I said quietly to myself between sips, basking in low-level ecstasy.

As author Roald Dahl lay dying of cancer on the 23rd of November 1990, surrounded by loved ones, he whispered to them, "It's just that I will miss you all so much." Dahl was not afraid of death and wanted to reassure those around him that neither should they be. And so, these were the perfect (*almost*) last words of one of the greatest children's writers that ever lived for, as everyone sat quietly by his side, a nurse injected Dahl with a needle, to which he responded with, "Ow, fuck!" before promptly dying.

Another interesting example of famous last words are not famous for the words themselves, but rather because they are completely unknown. When Albert Einstein died in New Jersey on the 18th of April 1955, his last words, according to his nurse, were, "something German". Since she couldn't speak German, she could not understand them, and thus, the last words of arguably the greatest mind of the 20th century were lost forever. If you are wondering why I am talking about famous last words on earth, it is because "this is going well!" could have easily been my own. It was after around two hours of walking after the rest stop that I realised I had gone a long time without seeing anything by way of a trail marker, be it a seashell or spray-painted arrow. Had

I skipped giddily past a fork in the road, leaving The Way completely? During my research for the trip, I repeatedly read how the route was so well marked, Stevie Wonder couldn't get lost. Yet here I was, at a crossroad both physically and metaphorically. My choice was simple. I could either take my medicine and backtrack for the next two hours to the point where I knew beyond doubt that I was back on the Camino, or I could choose to continue forwards down one of the three paths before me, even though I could safely assume at least two of them were wrong. *Fuck it,* I thought, doubling down by choosing the path straight ahead. After a further 90 minutes of walking almost entirely uphill, I was certain I had chosen the wrong option, a conclusion hastened by the most stifling heat I had walked in so far. At this point, I estimated that I was at least four hours from The Way, completely out of food, and the now laughably small water bottle I had chosen had long run dry. The sun was beating down on me unabated, with nowhere to take shade and, while I couldn't be sure if this Camino was bringing me closer to God, I was certain that it was bringing me closer to death. An extra option to the ones at the crossroad swiftly entered my mind — take out my pen and paper and leave a note next to my soon-to-be expired body (*Walked the Camino and all I got was this early grave!* was the best I could come up with). After another hour or so of zombie-like movement, I finally spotted signs of civilisation through a small cluster of trees. So desperate was I to beeline for them, I completely left the path I had put my trust in and made straight for a group of houses, dismissive of the treacherous off-road conditions. Somehow reaching them unharmed, I rapped firmly on the first front door I reached and, answering me, was a tiny old woman who must have been ninety if she was a day. Unsurprisingly, she didn't have a word of English in her head. Still, desperation must be a universal language, for it was not long until she understood the pickle I was in. She motioned me to wait and turned back into the house, returning soon after with a portly young man who I assumed to be her grandson. His name was Mateo, and his English was marginally better than my Spanish and, between us, I managed to successfully put across the reason for which I was darkening his door. I would have been eternally grateful to receive a mere point in the right direction and these people had done me a great kindness by just answering the door. When I asked Mateo how far I was from the Camino, he did that sharp intake of breath that mechanics do when they are about to give you a huge quote to fix your car. My heart sank. I had been on the road for over seven hours and was potentially still no way near my bag. The explanation seemed to be more trouble for Mateo that it was worth as, to my relief, he instead offered to drive me to Los Arcos (and crucially, back to The Way), after which it would be about an hour's walk to my stopping point of Sansol. Before we left, his alleged grandmother gave me plenty of water to drink and sent me on my way with an enormous crate of cherries, something I assumed the farming of which to be their livelihood. As I gratefully ate and drank, Mateo bizarrely took the opportunity to thank me personally for the existence of The Sex Pistols, about whom he waxed lyrically as if I was Johnny Rotten himself. When it was time to leave, Mateo beckoned me towards a souped-up Toyota Corolla that looked like it had been built based on a child's drawing, expertly swiping away the mountain of rubbish on the passenger seat. As we pulled slowly out of the driveway, his ancient granny tottered over to my side of the car. I rolled down the window, through which she thrust a small picture of the Virgin Mary, attempting no explanation for doing so. I thanked her anyway, to which she gave a sweet "Buen Camino", which at least filled in a few blanks.

After skilfully slaloming down the dirt track and onto the highway, Jewardo floored it, and we were in Los Arcos about fifteen minutes later. Leaving nothing to chance, he made sure to drop me off at a waymarker, triumphantly dodging the money I tried to give him for his help. Mateo too, wished me a hearty "Buen Camino" and, just like that, my new friend and I were parted. I sat on a public bench and hungrily ate the cherries without seeming to even make a dent in their volume before attempting to do the same to the remaining miles with renewed vigour.

I wasn't sure exactly where in Los Arcos I was, but the place seemed eerily quiet. At a modest population of around 1200, you wouldn't expect the streets to be swarming with bodies, but this low number belies what the town has to offer, particularly for fans of Romanesque, Baroque and Gothic architecture. I would have dearly loved to have explored the town thoroughly, but it was well into the late afternoon, and I really needed to get some serious walking done. As I was winding my way out of Los Arcos, I passed a cemetery on which the inscription at the gate reads,

"Yo que fui lo que tu eres, tu seras lo que yo soy". This translates into English as, "I was once what you are, and you will be what I am", which cheered me up no end.

Within an hour and a half, I had turned off the trail and was in Sansol, but the hotel I would supposedly find my bags wasn't. I went around the tiny village of no more than a couple of dozen houses without seeing any hotel, let alone the specific one I was looking for. Eventually, I found the sole town bar, where I attempted to ask the confounded bartender where the Hotel Yerri was. His furrowed brow caused me to lose a little hope, but his admission that there was no such place in Sansol was the coup de grâce. A quick internet search from the barman confirmed something interesting — there was a hotel by that name, but it wasn't in Sansol. It was, in fact, in Estrella, the town I just spent nearly 9 hours meandering away from. Jake had mistakenly (I hope) given me the hotel he was already at instead of the one he was staying at next. I hastily called the Hotel Yerri in Estrella, and lo and behold, there was my bag. While I had walked nearly 45 miles, my bags had moved just a hundred feet from my hotel to Jake's.

Taking mercy on me, the bartender called the taxi company and arranged for the bag to be brought out to where I actually was before sharing a good laugh at my expense with the other patrons. To be honest, I didn't care — I knew where my stuff was, and soon I would be reunited with it.

I ordered a much-needed drink and turned away from the bar to see Bernard, the German fellow from last night, soaking his feet in what looked like a cross between a foot spa and a children's paddling pool. I decided to join him and put my feet in also while I told him my tale. As we chatted in-depth on various topics, Bernard explained how this was the third time he had walked the Camino Frances. This fact seemed stranger the longer he talked, as it became more apparent that he didn't seem to know much about the places he was finding himself in every day, despite having been in them on multiple occasions. I was keen to complete a spoiler-free Camino, so I decided not to press the issue. Judging on the way Bernard described his experiences, it was clear that he favoured walking with a lighter load and very much enjoyed the finer things on offer for the modern pilgrim-about-town. His mission each day was fairly simple and usually worked the same — he would seek out the finest, most expensive hotel to lay his hat in whichever town he strode into. Based on Bernard's standards, many albergues would probably receive a negative number of stars, but there was usually at least one hotel in the 4 or 5-star range in most towns that he was able to sniff out like a fart in a lift. Failure to do so was a cause for concern tonight, however, as Bernard's look turned distinctly forlorn when the topic of that night's sleeping arrangements came up. As he lamented that his hotel for the evening was the holder of a measly 3-star rating, I nodded along, feigning grave concern, until a familiar face walked in. Seconds later, I was shaking hands with Raul, the spindly man I had seen take my bag that morning. He remarked via the barman's translation that he did think it was strange for someone to pay to have their bag taken from a hotel in one town to another one in the same town. After a celebratory drink with Raul, the barman pointed me toward the village's only guest house, which I made for without delay. The lodging was run by a lovely lady called Anna, who had repurposed the home her parents had left her when they passed away as a refuge for pilgrims. As I was checking-in in what I assume used to be a living room, I tried to remove the pilgrim passport from my money belt. The button on my trousers duly flew off, causing them to fall down to my ankles in front of this poor woman, successfully achieving my embarrassment quota for the day. She took this accidental exposure with good humour, by which I mean with roars of laughter, before ushering me out the back to the patio while she prepared my room. And who should I meet but Jake? Feet up, cigar in mouth, he asked,

"What took you so long?"

After regaling the story to him and Peter, Jake apologised for the mixup through stifled laughter before we all enjoyed the best meal of the Camino so far, as the home away from home atmosphere Anna provided the perfect end to the worst day. As it happened, this was the hotel Bernard was so reluctant to stay at. Given the town's small scale, I surmised it was probably his only choice, as he shifted unenthusiastically to the only remaining chair at the dinner table. Our final flatmate for the evening was a middle-aged Spanish man named Alejandro who, despite speaking no English, engaged gamely with the rest of us. Even Bernard was able to enjoy himself in the end.

12

SOUL'D SHORT

||||||||||||||||||||||||||||||||||||||||||||||||||||||||||||||||||||

A VALUABLE LESSON learnt, Estella would be the first and last time my bag was out of my sight. Walking without a bag just didn't feel right anyway. I did make the change from boots to sandals a permanent one, however, and if I was to compile a list of top tips for walking the Camino, this one would be at the very top. The boots were causing more injuries than they were preventing in my case and, by switching to sandals, less material was in contact with the foot, meaning a reduction in blister-caused chafing. Add this to the fact that virtually no point of the Camino has such rough terrain as to require the most robust footwear on the market, it was probably the best mid-Camino decision I made.

While I was at it, there were some other accessories I didn't need, starting with that bloody guidebook. Before leaving Manchester, I had read that thing cover to cover and felt as if the wool had been pulled over my eyes. I had been taken for a ride. Hoodwinked. Bamboozled. Flimflammed. Not only were the distances quoted highly dubious, but so were some of the suggestions for stopping points. I sensed that I had been taken in by something that was, in essence, telling me what to think. Perhaps I had a latent desire to not be surprised by what I would encounter because it might provide me with a challenge and, in turn, potential discomfort. Before taking a single step on Camino, I knew the best places to stay, eat and see. I held a desire for the excitement of a rugged adventure as long as it was safe, clean and as close to free as possible. The honest truth is that it didn't have to be rugged. It just needed to appear so to everyone else. I wasn't an explorer, I was a pilgrim. We all were. All of us were subject to the same risk and reward for our individual decisions in choosing to walk. I craved adventure yet somehow feared it. I took the simple and over-complicated it before becoming exasperated at its lack of simplicity. I was demanding more of myself in an already demanding situation. As I threw that thing in the next bin I came across, I made a mental note to punch one of these writers in the nose if I ever met one.

Guidebook aside, I think I did a decent job in packing for a trip I had never done the likes of before, regardless of not everything I brought being essential. I was now doubly glad I didn't listen to my colleague when she tried to persuade me to bring with me some genuinely useless stuff, such as a screwdriver. Not as part of a Swiss Army knife; a regular screwdriver you might find in a toolbox. Pound-for-pound, the earplugs were probably the best purchase I made in terms of the Camino (if not my entire life) when roommates are a consideration. Ever since I slept in bunk beds with my older brother as a child, sharing a room has always been bothersome. Snoring, farting, coughing — I couldn't do any of it in the albergues. Multiply all those things by a factor of fifty in some instances, and you are highly unlikely to get consecutive minutes of silence that you can count on one hand. Be that as it may, towards the end of the journey, falling asleep amongst the pilgrim 'white noise' did get easier with time. Perhaps I should have recorded it to reminisce over should I ever long for the memory since half of it was probably my own.

I never saw Anna again but awoke in the morning to find she had left a magnificent continental breakfast out for us all, which was soon devoured with gusto. Alejandro set off first, followed by Bernard a few minutes later. Jake and Peter dawdled somewhat, so I decided to head on without them, sure their unrestricted frames would catch up with me before long. Back on the trail, the next village of Torres del Rio is so close, you could fall out of bed in Sansol to find yourself halfway there and, if Sansol is sleepy, then Torres del Rio is positively comatose, with the most famous thing either town is renowned for being the fact that they stand opposite to one another. A thigh-burning 10-kilometre climb awaits anyone still awake after leaving the latter, with the small town of Viana being the next place of significance.

Getting lost may have been one of the more unnerving incidents of my Camino, if not my whole life, but at least it made for a good story. A touch of the supernatural wouldn't have gone amiss, though. After all, who doesn't enjoy a good ghost story? Ever since I was a child, trembling as I listened to tales of the banshee in rural Ireland from my grandmother, I have enjoyed being scared. Whether it be movies, stories or podcasts — anything spooky that I can get my hands, ears or eyes on is sure to entertain. Much of my recent attraction to this genre is rooted in local folklore, such as the banshee — a female spirit from Irish mythology whose horrifying cry heralds the imminent death of the hearer's loved one. It would appear that Santiago, the terminus of the Camino and capital of Galicia, is rich in such myth and legend, even today. For instance, the Costa de Morte or "Death Coast", which stretches from Finisterre northwards to Malpica, owes its reputation to English sailors in the 15th century for being an area blighted with frequent shipwrecks due to dangerous and challenging sea conditions. Since Roman times, Finisterra was considered the end of the world and was held highly by pagans and pre-Christians alike. To these people, the sun vanished under the sea, connecting the living world with that of the dead. Large rocks, known locally as holy or oscillating stones, can be found in the area, the most famous of which, "Pedras de abalar", is in Muxía. Legend has it that this stone was once part of a boat that carried the Virgin Mary to visit St James, although evidence exists that this and other stones were worshipped in a pre-Christian era. It was believed that, since these stones could move or make noise without being touched, they were credible in predicting events like shipwrecks or even determining one's guilt, as well as possessing healing powers.

Now one thing you may want to avoid on Camino is something you ultimately won't be able to — crossroads. For it is here where you might run afoul of the Santa Compaña, the dreaded procession of dead souls, believed to frequent crossings on Galicia's numerous country lanes. Special nights such as Halloween are supposed to make a sighting more likely but, unfortunately for me, so was mid-summer, making the crossing of our paths virtually guaranteed. By noticing that this book does not end here, you will have correctly deduced that this did not happen. This was just as well since, at the time, I wouldn't have known to draw a circle around myself to prevent my abduction. Or to not accept the candle they would indeed offer me for, if I had, I would have been doomed to haunt the lanes of Galicia for eternity. For this reason, so many stone crosses (or cruceiros) can be found at crossroads all over Galicia, hampering the recruitment efforts of this army of the damned. If you would prefer to make doubly sure of avoiding such a terrible fate, look out for the 'petos de ánimas' or 'soul pockets' that can sometimes be found at crossroads. It is into these that offerings to the poor souls stuck there can be put, hastening their time in purgatory before their ascension into heaven. Now, if all else fails, you still have the option to fight fire with fire or spirit with spirit, to be more precise. Take a swig of

Queimada, a drink made from a combination of Galician spirits, lemon peel, coffee beans and sugar. It might sound disgusting, but apparently, lighting it while reciting a spell makes it a potent punch for a poltergeist.

Upon arrival in Santiago, be sure to visit Quintana square around the back of the magnificent cathedral and pay homage to its 'invisible' residents. You will immediately notice that the court is split in half by a set of stairs, dividing the Quintana dos Vivos (Quintana of the living) from the Quintana dos Mortos (Quintana of the dead). With any luck, you might catch a glimpse of the shadow of a pilgrim that is said to appear in one corner of the latter every night. Or perhaps you will visit Bonaval Park, the relaxing green space next to the convent at San Domingos de Bonaval. That is, if you find sitting on the site of a late 18th-century burial ground to be your idea of relaxation. The legend of the Shadow of the Pilgrim is arguably the most well-known Camino-related ghost story. It tells the story of a priest from the cathedral in Santiago and a nun from the nearby Monastery of San Paio de Antealtares who fell in love, regularly holding clandestine meetings in the underground passageway linking the two. The priest wished for them to leave their life of religious service behind and run off together, suggesting that they meet in the town square of Plaza del Obradoiro that night. When nightfall came, the priest arrived disguised as a pilgrim to not arouse suspicion but, sadly for him, his lover never did. He is still said to haunt the spot at the clock's base beside the Holy Gate every night, awaiting his beloved.

Away from the Land of the Dead, the municipality of Viana can be seen from the plains long before it is reached. The town is the result of an amalgamation of eight villages by Sancho VII (also known as Sancho the Strong) in 1219 that were all built atop an originally Roman settlement. Like many towns of the time, strong (pun intended), fortified walls are a prominent feature, indicating the town's significance, particularly to the kingdoms of Navarre and Castille, who took turns occupying it. Arguably the most prominent figure in the history of Viana is Cesare Borgia of the infamous House of Borgia, an Italian politician and military commander who happened to be the illegitimate son of Pope Alexander VI. In 1490, Borgia became the Bishop of Pamplona at the tender age of 15, eventually becoming a Cardinal when his father assumed the Papacy, becoming the first man in history to resign from that office in 1490. From there, he served as a Captain in the army of King Louis XII of France in several campaigns during the Great Wars of Italy.

After the death of his father (followed by the 26-day reign of Pious III), Cesare's fortunes took a turn for the worse when his enemy, Giuliano Della Rovere, was elected Pope Julius II in 1503, and the Papal support he had enjoyed was withdrawn. Subsequently imprisoned in Italy and then Spain, Borgia managed to escape and fled to Pamplona, where he was gratefully received by King John III of Navarre. John lacked the military leadership that Borgia possessed to capture the nearby municipality of Viana, something the latter would go on to deliver in 1507. While laying siege to the castle, Borgia was isolated from his army and ambushed by a group of knights, killing him.

Borgias's epitaph read as follows:

Here lies in a little earth
he who everyone feared,
he who peace and war
held in his hand.

Oh, you who go in search
of worthy things to praise,
if you would praise the worthiest
then your path stops here
and you do not need to go any farther.

Although the words above are something we could expect John III to have used when talking about Borgia, whom he greatly respected, the reality is that these words were actually written in the 18th century. Cesare Borgia was initially buried at the altar of the Church of Santa Maria in Viana on the orders of John III, only for his bones to be dug up and reburied several times until they found their final resting place outside of the church in 1953. Ironically, Borgia could not be reburied inside the church because of a church ruling against such a thing for anyone other than popes or cardinals. Since he had renounced his cardinalate, he was ultimately disqualified from such an honour.

I waved goodbye to not only Viana, but the province of Navarre as the trail undulated gently over and under busy roads, making way for the vineyards and olive groves that would take me to the autonomous community of Rioja. My next overnight stop would be the capital of the region, Logroño, situated on the banks of the Ebro river. The trail took me straight into the town centre, leaving me spoilt for choice for accommodation. I was determined not to make the same mistake by wandering aimlessly searching for a bed as I had in Pamplona, and so opted for an agreeable-looking hotel with cafes and restaurants close at hand that had a small hotel bar if I didn't feel like going out.

The progressive measures set out in the charter granted to Logroño in 1095 by King Alphonso VI would set the tone for future covenants throughout the Kingdom of Castille. Under it, forced labour of the peasantry was outlawed, as were unfair taxes and restrictions of access to fertile land. These actions ensured that Logroño flourished, making it highly coveted by neighbouring kingdoms. Originally an old Roman settlement named Varea, Logroño has spent time over the centuries as part of the Kingdoms of Navarre and Castille and, despite being well away from the region, the site of the Basque Witch trials of 1609 that formed part of the Spanish Inquisition. With a population of over 150,000, the vibrant university town is the largest urban centre in Rioja and the beating heart of the region's world-famous wine industry. Logroño is also home to the magnificent Concatedral de Santa María de la Redonda. With its ornate pair of identical towers, each containing its own set of bells, you will find three clock faces, one each for the hour, the minute and the second. High iron gates and netting have been placed in the alcove to protect the sculptures from people and birds respectively, save for the most elevated ledges of the towers, on which the native storks can still perch. Another must-see is the Fuente de la Gran Vía, where bronze statues of royal figures can be found. The statues are known locally as 'wet backs' due to the fact they have been placed looking out towards the public as the water pours down behind them.

Much like Pamplona, Logroño is teeming with parks, plazas and restaurants in a vibrant social scene. Known as the "path of the elephants", Calle de Laurel offers some of the best food in northern Spain. While walking along the street, I noticed that almost every bar and restaurant that I passed displayed small slices of bread on top of which various ingredients were held in place by a toothpick. When hunger and curiosity eventually forced me to partake in some, a friendly and knowledgeable waiter informed me that these creations were called 'pinchos' (and most definitely not tapas), so-called because of the "spike" holding it together.

After a half dozen or so pinchos, I looked off into the middle distance to see Trevor and Leanne strolling hand in hand in my general direction. Happy to see them for the first time in a few days, I thrust my hand in the air as one might summon a taxi in an attempt to catch their attention, only to be soon cut off by a handful of over-attentive waiters. Whether it was the bustling posse of white shirts that got their attention rather than my limp wrist, it mattered not, as we were all soon the worse for drink and hoarse from laughter. Since they were the only married couple I had seen on Camino until that point, I pressed them on why they had chosen it for a holiday. Trevor was a successful lawyer and Leanne a midwife, and both were in their mid-forties with the couple's 15-year-old son deciding to stay with school friends in Scotland. While I could understand that the Camino would not be a choice holiday for a teenager, I wondered why these parents would prefer rambling through Spain over a more conventional family holiday. Trevor anticipated this and put forth a much less profound reason than I expected. Leanne's brother had some years earlier married a girl from the Basque region and now resided there with his young family. After deciding to visit, Trevor and Leanne were researching the area when they learned about the Camino, deciding it would be fun to walk a section simultaneously. Leanne's brother now lived about 5km south of Logroño, to where they would take a bus to finish their vacation. This sadly meant their Camino was now over, as was now the case for virtually all the crowd from Scotland that I had become so fond of.

In terms of motivation, walking the Camino de Santiago because it was on the way to visit a sibling was an exception. To me, it came as no surprise that, like myself, most pilgrims I met prefaced their rationale for pilgrimage by mentioning that they first heard of it on a movie or TV show. Of course, the more popular something becomes, pop culture eventually takes notice. The Camino has been covered in plenty of television series over the years, but more recently in the Martin Sheen film I touched on earlier, The Way. The plot of the film centres around an American doctor named Tom (Sheen), who learns of his estranged son Daniel's (Estevez) tragic death in a storm attempting to cross the Pyrenees during the opening stage of the Camino de Santiago. Initially travelling to St Jean to retrieve his son's remains for repatriation, Tom has a change of heart and cremates his son's body before attempting the walk on his behalf, spreading his son's ashes as he goes. As the film progresses, Tom becomes profoundly impacted by the journey and the people he meets. Inexperienced in hiking, Tom is initially determined to walk solo, becoming resentful of his fellow pilgrims, before learning to tolerate them and ultimately enjoying, perhaps even depending on them. The supporting cast of characters all have differing reasons for walking, but all seek meaning in their lives and hope that the Camino will provide it. Accompanying Tom for the majority of his journey are Dutchman, Joost (played by Yorick van Wageningen), who is walking the Camino to lose weight, Canadian, Sarah (played by Deborah Kara Unger), who is recently out of an abusive relationship and Jack (played by James Nesbitt), an Irish writer amid a debilitating period of 'writer's block'. Along the way, the group forms an enjoyable (albeit predictable) bond, as Tom grieves while learning to understand what his son meant by saying, "the difference between the life we live and the life we choose".

However, the 2010 film was not the first silver screen portrayal of the Camino. Surrealist and Salvador Dali collaborator Luis Buñuel used The Way as the central plot to his 1969 film, The Milky Way, taking aim at the filmmaker's perceived dogma of the Catholic church. In 2003, British art critic Brian Sewell produced a documentary in which he travelled The Way on a journey of spiritual rediscovery while providing insights on the breathtaking art and architecture along the route, culminating at the feast of St James in Santiago. In 2005 French comedy, *Saint Jacques... La Mecque*, three siblings with mutual loathing for one another must make a joint pilgrimage to Santiago in order to inherit their late mother's wealth.

After wishing Trevor and Leanne a fond farewell, I headed back to my hotel and, on the way, ran into Jake and Peter while they were on their usual stroll to nowhere in particular. Remembering the small hotel bar, I extended an invitation for them to join me for a nightcap, and the next thing I knew, all three of us were propping up the bar. Jake and Peter were both expected home by their wives the next day and were heading north to Bilbao airport in the morning. When I learned the ungodly hour they needed to rise in order to catch the coach, I was astonished they would choose to be drinking with me instead of getting an early night — particularly Peter, who boasted about the fact he had still not done a hint, note or suggestion of any packing. This was in total contrast to Jake, who lectured extensively on various packing techniques and the situations in which they should be applied.

Part-way through Jake's seminar on rolling clothes to save space, Peter remembered the telescopic walking pole he would not be taking home since it was stuck in its extended position, meaning there was no way to fit it in his backpack. He kindly said I could have it, sagely advising that one in each hand would help me cover ground more efficiently, reducing the risk of injury. Circling his hotel on a map of downtown, Peter promised to leave the pole in reception, from where I could collect it tomorrow morning. After finally being convinced by Jake to go there himself to start packing, the pair asked me to keep them posted on my exploits en route to Santiago before leaving me to it. And by 'it', I hope they meant 'go to bed', because that is what I did.

13

POULTRY IN MOTION

||||||||||||||||||||||||||||||||||||||||||||||||||||||||||||||||||||||||||||||||||||||||||||||||||||||||||

I WOKE UP the next morning fully clothed and hungover, glancing over at the bedside clock to see it was 9:30, no less than 90 minutes since I should have checked out. Since I hadn't been woken by an angry bellhop, I assumed this wasn't a problem for the hotel, but it certainly was for me. By now, I should have been walking for nearly 3 hours which, by my estimate, would put me over halfway to my next stopping point of Nájera. Setting off late has the potential to cause problems for a pilgrim if they arrive at a destination to find affordable accommodation already booked up, a problem I could do without. As I prepared to leave, I reproached myself for staying up late to get drunk when I could ill afford it, lamenting the already hot weather that would surely dehydrate me even more than the alcohol already had. As I made my way out of Logroño, my brain felt as if it was falling apart like a piece of wet cake, so I stopped at a small convenience store to pick up something for breakfast and some much-needed water to clear the fog in my pounding head. Feeling reinvigorated, I bade Logroño adios as I passed through the city gate of

Puerta del Camino, built by Carlos V in the early 16th century, ready to get my head down and power through the next 27km.

About halfway between Logroño and Najera is the town of Navarette. It was here I abandoned any hope of catching up to where I would have been had it not been for my self-inflicted lateness and took a much-needed break to refuel. Psychologically, I found it essential to only stop for rest once I was at least halfway to my next bed and, with this now achieved for today, already felt better for it. The second walking pole Jake had left me with did the world of good. Having another to balance out the first helped enormously as the strain on my knees was now shared equally. With no need to alternate one solitary pole between hands every few miles, my arms were now helping instead of dangling inefficiently by my sides. Adequately rested, I hauled myself from under the shade of a tree and pushed on towards Najera via the village of Ventosa.

Much of the trail leading to Ventosa stays close to the busy N120 highway, which I was pleased for. It gave my ears something to listen to as my eyes feasted on the region's local vineyards and red clay that I had to brush off myself more than a few times. The village covers less than 4 square miles and is a place that no more than 200 people call home but was a welcome break from the afternoon heat as I filled up my (new and much larger) water bottle. While nothing of note is in the village, the ruined monastery of San Anton can be seen as you leave, albeit considerably off the trail. The site of the fallen monastery is said to be close to the spot where legendary Saracen giant Ferragus was defeated by Roland, but with no time or inclination for detours, I attacked the last 8km to Najera instead.

As I entered the former capital of the Kingdom of Navarre, I stopped the first pilgrim I saw to find the town's municipal hostel as soon as possible and was directed towards the Najerilla river, just over which the albergue could be found. I made for it with haste, believing my chances of finding a free bed to be slim to none. I arrived to find the reception bustling but, since I was a solitary pilgrim yet to check-in, I fit the last remaining bed like the proverbial hand in glove. Amongst the gaggle was a small posse of Germans, who all gleefully approached me as if I were a celebrity, confounding me thoroughly. When someone addresses you, yet you have no idea who they are, there is a very small window during which a choice from the following must be made;

Option 1: Admit straight away that you haven't the foggiest idea who they are.

Option 2: Play along in a desperate attempt to remember who they are.

Option 3: Ask probing questions hoping they will reveal who they are.

Option 4: Take too long to choose from the options above and stare blankly mouth agape.

My choice of Option 4 caused mirth aplenty in their ranks. It transpired that I had somewhat of a fan club and, after seeing me in passing several times, I learned that they had affectionately dubbed me 'Unicorn Man' due to the unicorn keyring that my wife had attached to my bag on the day I left England. There were two women, Heike and Valarie and one man, Rene, who at 7 foot 1 inch tall, was the closest thing to a fairytale giant that I had ever encountered. As his voice boomed, I imagined him scooping up pilgrims by the armful, stepping over mountains in a single bound. Heike was a lovely girl who had an adorable squint as if the sun was perpetually in her eyes, and Valarie introduced herself to me by sticking her middle finger up in front of my face because she thought it was hilarious that, a few seconds earlier, a bird had shit directly on it. Kindly, they invited me to join them for dinner that evening and, with my bed for the night secured, I gratefully accepted.

With a population of around 9000, Najera hits that sweet spot where one can find enough to keep themselves interested, but not too much as to overload the senses or so spread out as to make seeing everything impossible. At least on paper it did. It was about 4pm and, without dinner plans until 7, I had time for some learning. Firstly, Najera has the dubious honour of being the first *titular see* that I have ever visited (to my knowledge). Although it sounds like an ancient Roman gentleman's club, the term actually refers to a catholic diocese that no longer functions, a status established here in 1969. For this reason, I thought there would be a fighting chance that I could visit something of note that wasn't a church for a change, but I was out of luck. However, the church of Santa Maria la Real, whose origins date back to the 11th century, is still worth a visit for the remarkable gothic-style wood carving in the choir, if nothing else.

When Najera became the capital of Navarre towards the end of the 10th century, the Camino was subsequently diverted in order to pass through the town. The influx of pilgrims (along with the money they brought) significantly increased the fortunes of Najera, and it experienced an upturn in ecclesiastical prominence as a result. However, by the 16th century, pilgrim numbers had diminished significantly, causing monasteries like Santa Maria to fall into disrepair. The monastery's prosperity was revived with the arrival of the Franciscans in the late 19th century who still maintain the church today. As with just about every city, town, village and hamlet I have encountered on this journey, Najera was originally Roman (then known as Tritium), after which it existed under Muslim rule (deriving its name from Arabic meaning *town between the rocks*), before being conquered in the name of Christianity by the Kingdom of Navarre, then by the Kingdom of Castille for some other self-indulgent reason. With little else to do after visiting the monastery, I spent a while sitting on the freshly cut grass by the river before heading back to the hostel to relax on my bunk bed.

I arrived at the restaurant next door a few minutes early to find the gang already there, after which we ate, talked and shared about our lives and our personal reasons for walking the Camino. On the table next to ours was a twenty-something Italian man I had noticed a few times since Saint-Jean, attempting to flirt with a young Korean woman. What made this chap memorable was that every time I saw him on the trail, he was running instead of walking and, the more I thought about it, the more I wondered how I kept catching him up. After all, I wasn't walking particularly far or fast, so why were we covering the same distances? The young lady took to his seduction technique like a duck to concrete and soon left him in his own company to lick his wounds. With plenty of chairs, good cheer and sympathy to spare, I invited him to sit with us. He introduced himself to us as Mario and, when asked, explained that he simply ran the trail to reach stopping points sooner, leaving himself more time for exploration of the fairer sex. Mario was terrific fun and the living embodiment of if at first you don't succeed, try again in the next town. I, for one, was rooting for him to whittle down pilgrims in his search for a potential mate by the time he set foot in Santiago.

After dinner, we headed back to the albergue to find something of a kerfuffle in reception. Jason, the Nutella wholesaler I met on the first day, was in the centre of a mass of jostling pilgrims, all eager to make their case to the hospitalero behind the desk. As I mentioned earlier, the last remaining bed went to yours truly, yet here was Jason, flanked by a dozen advocates, pleading to be given a bed for the night. At almost 10 O'Clock, the doors were not just closed to new guests, they were about to be locked to everyone whether you were in the book or not. After a brief earwig, I learned that someone had decided to relieve Jason of his tent — unfortunate proof that even those on pilgrimage were still vulnerable to pilfering. Notwithstanding, it still took persistent nagging from the other pilgrims to secure Jason a space on the floor that night. Once the matter was settled, I spent a few minutes chatting with Jason in the small communal area while his sleeping space was being prepared. As I was commiserating him for his lousy stroke of luck, he politely interrupted me by smiling while waving his hand in a dismissive motion, explaining that he bore the thief no ill will. At first glance, Jason could be considered an eccentric character — a free spirit, you might say. He bathed in rivers and lakes, ate and drank whatever he could for free and slept under the stars with nothing but a tent in between. Until tonight, my only interaction with him had been over that lifetime supply of hazelnut spread on day one. I had seen him fleetingly on occasion since, yet had unfairly judged his character based on the observations I just gave, and now I felt as if I was only now truly meeting him. After dinner, I had had my fill of listening to other peoples' reasons for walking but was now hopeful Jason would share his. While the lion's share (including my own) were vapid and uninspired, Jason's was particularly sorrowful. Less than a year before he stepped his first from Saint-Jean, Jason had lost his teenage son to a rare genetic illness and was walking the Camino to help him work through the grief. A wave of shame washed over me for my earlier feelings of self-pity over blistered feet or an uncomfortable mattress when this poor man had gone through something no one should by burying his own child. The love and compassion that he showed for his fellow pilgrims, even the thieving ones, without a word of complaint for the hand life had dealt him, was a testament to the resolve the human spirit is capable of.

I woke up nice and early the following morning, ready to hit the ground running. I had gone to bed the night before in what I had worn to dinner, an act of laziness that had inadvertently prepared me to get walking immediately, and I did so with relish. I stepped out of the albergue into the cool Spanish morning to meet Heike and Valarie, who were smoking on the benches that ran along the outside wall. With no bags in their vicinity and looking half-asleep, I knew they were nowhere near ready to walk and so promised to catch up with them 25km away in Santo Domingo de la Calzada, if not sooner.

I headed behind the Santa Maria church I had visited yesterday to rejoin the trail, mainly heading uphill through pine forest and luscious greenery, reaching the fun-sized village of Azofra about an hour and a half later. Since the sun had barely caught me still in bed, I was flummoxed to see a dozen or so pilgrims apparently taking a break from walking. However unlikely, I suppose it is entirely possible that these pilgrims had spent the night here yet found themselves fatigued this soon in the day. As I strode past them (all the while staring in their direction like a madman), it appeared to be the only explanation since I had enjoyed the last 10km to myself, having been overtaken by no one. I left them to savour their coffee, in total confidence at least one of them would jot down my appearance in case an e-fit was ever needed.

Ten or so kilometres later, I entered the even smaller village of Cirueña. Now what made this place significant was the fact that passing through it was entirely optional. While crossing the N120 highway, I glimpsed a trio of pilgrims intentionally ignoring the waymarkers, favouring the road to reach Santo Domingo directly, avoiding Cirueña altogether. While there was no way I would do anything other than stick religiously to the signage after the debacle of Sansol, skipping a village, however small, felt like cheating to me. Not wishing for an asterisk to be put next to my name in Santiago, I put my thighs to good use and climbed to Cirueña, where I took the weight off my feet for a period before the last push downhill to the market town of Santo Domingo.

Located on the banks of the River Oja, Santo Domingo is named after the 11th century Saint Dominic of the Causeway in celebration of the numerous ways he aided pilgrims en route to Santiago, including the building of a bridge, a hostel and a church (that would eventually become a cathedral) at which his remains are interred. Born the son of a peasant in 1019, Dominic came into the world just outside the town that bears his name in the village of Viloria de Rioja. After being rejected twice by the Benedictine order, he retreated into a life of hermitage in the forests of Ayuela until he was 20 years old. From here, he travelled to Calahorra, about 50km south of Estella, to work under the bishop of Ostia, Gregory IV, who had been sent from Rome as a papal envoy to deal with the plague of locusts rampaging through La Rioja and Navarre. As a reward, Dominic was ordained a priest by Gregory before the two set about building a wooden bridge that would be used to help pilgrims cross the Oja while on Camino. When Gregory passed away in 1044, Domingo returned to the forest with his own apprentice in Juan de Ortega to clear the trees in which he once found solitude, replacing them with a causeway (hence, Calzada), linking the towns that I now found myself between, Logroño and Burgos. Soon removed thereafter was the wooden bridge he built with Gregory to be replaced with a stone one. Not content with this, the pair also went on to build a pilgrim hostel that still stands today, the Casa del Santo. Domingo was able to complete a vast amount of works until his death in 1109, partly thanks to the patronage of the Castilian king, Alfonso VI, after the latter annexed the Rioja region in 1076. Towards the end of his life, the town I was now walking through was little more than a handful of houses, yet the population continued to grow due to the strong foundations he built, culminating in his church being elevated to the status of cathedral in 1230. I was amused to learn that one of the miracles attributed to Domingo was the restoration of a German pilgrim's eyesight in the fifteenth century. What grabbed my interest was the man's name,

Bernard. Since the Bernard I knew also wore glasses, he surely had nothing to lose by visiting Santa Domingo's tomb.

As I strolled along Calle Mayor in the heart of Santo Domingo, I was pleasantly surprised to meet Kevin and Michael, the father and son double act I first met in Roncesvalles. Kevin explained that he and his son decided to extend their pilgrimage beyond the planned seven days, with their new (and "100% definitely certain, Duncan") endpoint being Belorado, a day's walk from the chairs we were sitting in. However, due to flight schedules, they would be staying in Santo Domingo for an extra day before their final day on Camino the day after. While this meant that our paths had to split after only crossing again, I made sure to take down Kevin's contact information so I could stay in touch, something I would endeavour to do more often from then on. With the word "Goodbye" barely out of my mouth, I continued along the busy street to find myself walking straight into the outstretched arms of my favourite Nutella merchant, Jason. Jason seemed to be in a particularly good mood this afternoon, and we disengaged our embrace well before the widely accepted maximum of 20 seconds, after which Jason immediately looked beyond me to the person behind. I looked back and realised that I had inadvertently joined a procession of pilgrims that were about to do the same. While there was no way of knowing it at the time, Jason's Nutella-fueled hugging marathon would be my abiding memory of him, as that was the last I saw of the most wonderfully strange man I ever did meet. For all I know, he is still there.

As I sauntered around town, my appreciation for the relaxed atmosphere in the air grew, and I was impatient to be free of my backpack, so I could experience it more comfortably. For this reason, I checked into the first albergue that I spotted, something that I would live to regret. I approached the building and pushed and pulled the front door to find it did neither. In full view behind the desk was a haggard,

Mrs Mop type character who stared unflinchingly as I shook the door several times with our eyes locked. After an unsettling amount of time doing this, she checked the clock behind her before finally heaving herself out of the chair and traipsing over to let me in, struggling with the key as if her body was being remotely controlled from another room. When I got inside at long last, the lady apologised for letting me catch her daydreaming, explaining how she simply forgot to unlock the door. Her name was Mar, and she was a bubbly sort of lady in a way that totally belied her outwardly dour demeanour. As she completed the time-honoured tradition of stamping my credential during check-in, she did something else that every inn, hotel and hostel I had stayed at so far had done — take a photocopy of my passport. By now, I was overcome with curiosity and, since her English was excellent, asked her about it. Mar educated me that, in Spain, it is a legal requirement for innkeepers to keep a record of anyone who stays in their establishments. Although technically she was supposed to copy down the information from my passport, I didn't see the harm in letting her cut a corner by using an office photocopier that looked old enough to be haunted.

Mar offered to take my bag to the 'sleeping room' as soon as she had cleaned it, telling me with a knowing look to explore 'Santo' (as she called it) for another hour or two in the meantime. My exploring took me all of 20 feet to a cafe, where I thoroughly explored the menu and a bottle of house red. When I returned to the albergue a couple of hours later, Mar invited me to follow her through a small patio area to the back of the property. The room in which pilgrims slept was approximately the size of a large living room and contained at least a dozen bunk beds, all of which were now full, save for a bottom bunk in the corner, on which my bag lay. I laid down next to it, but after half an hour staring at the bulging mattress above me, I went back out to the patio area to find it empty, aside from Mar, who was half-heartedly wiping down the plastic tables and chairs.

I sat down at the one furthest away from her since it was the one most likely to be dry. As I did so, I instantly became self-conscious that this might unintentionally appear rude and so made sure to make some small talk from across the room. Mar seemed grateful for the distraction and abandoned her cleaning to join me right where I noted how much more tired she looked compared to when I first met her just a few hours ago. Mar explained that although the running of the albergue single-handedly under constant financial pressure was all-consuming, she was still happy with her lot in life. I think the chance to vent to someone who wasn't looking for a discount or to complain about something was a relief to her and, after only five minutes, she appeared revitalised for having done so. I can therefore deduce, it is for this reason she didn't detect me lying through my teeth when I said I had no complaints. Mar noticed the map of Santo I was fiddling with and asked me if I had discovered anything interesting after she had ordered me to do so. I confessed to being too lazy, hungry and fond of a drink to do so, expecting her to shake her head in disappointment and go back to rearranging the dust. On the contrary, her face lit up after hearing this, and she told me the story of *The Chickens of Santo Domingo de la Calzada* with delight.

As with many legends, this story is more akin to a 700-year long game of Chinese whispers than a factual narrative. It was about a German family who stopped for the night in Santo Domingo on their way to Santiago, seven centuries before myself. After their arrival, an unnamed local girl took a liking to Hugonell, the family's teenage son, but her feelings were not reciprocated. Feeling scorned, she planted a silver cup into the young man's bag before accusing him of stealing it. The town took her at her word, and brutal medieval justice was swiftly meted out, with the boy soon finding himself with a one-way ticket to the gallows. Amazingly, the poor lad's parents took this on the chin and continued their pilgrimage to Santiago, hopefully where they at least took time to pray for him. On their way back home from Santiago, they returned to Santo Domingo to visit their son to find him not only still hanging from the noose but inexplicably still alive. I suppose they were making such good time en-route to Santiago, they didn't want to waste any of it on trifling matters such as waiting to see their son breathe his last, let alone be buried. They did at least demand that he be cut down after what must have been several months hanging by his neck. Such demands were the responsibility of the magistrate in Santiago, who was just sitting down to enjoy chicken for dinner when they hurriedly arrived. Upon hearing the parents' request, he was heard to remark,

"That boy is no more alive than the chicken on my plate!"

Legend has it that as soon as those words passed his lips, the chicken jumped up off the plate, its feathers, beak and face back where they belonged. Upon seeing this, the shaken lawman promptly granted the young man a pardon and subsequent freedom. Spreading like the proverbial wildfire, the story of the chicken eventually led to a request from the townsfolk for papal permission to display carvings of a hen and a rooster inside the church in commemoration of the miracle. The proposal was granted.

Mar banged her hand on the table with such enthusiasm as she told the story that I wouldn't want to guess which would break first. While stories of people being saved from certain death are nothing new, the chicken element made this story two miracles for the price of one, something for which Mar seemed visibly proud. At this moment, I realised that it was the carvings in the cathedral that she wanted me to discover. When I asked her about this, she agreed, partly. In addition to the carvings, one rooster and one hen are kept alive in the cathedral all year round, making me doubly regretful for putting my stomach before seeing them. Like a bona fide half-wit, I asked if these were some sort of immortal fowl that were once on the menu of a magistrate, causing her to snort with laughter before explaining the chickens are replaced once a month and kept in a coop supported by donations. I wished Mar a good night and headed back to the room, praying that the others were asleep. They were.

14

HOTEL MY WIFI LOVE HER

||||||||||||||||||||||||||||||||||||||||||||||||||||||||||||||||||||||||||||||||||||||||||||||||||||||||||||||||||||||||||||||||||||||||||||||||||||||||||||||||

THE NEXT MORNING I opened my eyes to find most of the other nameless pilgrims I had shared the room with were gone. As those of us remaining packed up our belongings, I was sure that being late to my next stopping point of Belorado would be worth going to see the chickens for. As I made my way through to reception, Mar was waiting at her desk with a plateful of chicken-shaped biscuits called Milagros del Santo, meaning miracles of the Saint. She thrust the plate so close to my face, I could have picked one up with my lips if I had wanted to, but I opted instead to crane my neck back to get a better look before taking one from the pile. When I asked Mar if she had baked these herself, she blushed and shook her head, admitting she had collected them from the bakery that morning to give to her pellegrinos, although I didn't entirely believe her. I hoisted my bag and, with hearty "adios", left my sweet innkeeper with the rest of her milagrosas.

While making my way to the cathedral, I walked against the steady flow of pilgrims, feeling like a salmon swimming upstream. The metaphor was complete when Rene, the proverbial bear, flanked me with a literal bear hug while my head was buried in a map. The surprise caused me to nearly fall, and I would have if it were not for his brute strength, his arms lifting me up and towards him, leaving my legs to dangle as if I was a toddler in his mother's arms. Having narrowly avoided soiling myself, I regained my composure and told Rene of my plan to see the chickens in the cathedral before hiking to Belorado. Given that Valarie and Heike had already set off, Rene thought this was a capital idea and offered to take me there since he knew the way. Once I was sure that he meant he would show me the way, as opposed to literally picking me up and delivering me, off we went.

Rene and I paid our entry fee of €6, after which we were warned that taking pictures of the chickens was prohibited. As expected, however, we entered to find this rule roundly ignored by every living soul capable of using a camera. In any case, Mar was true to her word. There were unmistakably two chickens strutting around an ornately carved pen inside an actual cathedral. While I cannot fathom why photographing a chicken would be forbidden, I remained confident that no one would dare challenge me as long as the German Goliath was by my side. Deciding to respect the chickens' privacy regardless, I left the cathedral with nothing more than a lighter wallet and a useless memory. Rene and I opted not to explore the rest of the cathedral, agreeing instead to tackle the next stage of our Camino together.

Within minutes, we were proceeding down Calle Mayor for the final time, at last crossing the bridge you now all can't wait to tell your friends about. Back with a vengeance was our old friend, the N120 highway, alongside which we would spend much of the day walking, save for the occasional village or field. After about an hour, we reached the village of Grañón, the last one we would pass through on the Camino Frances before swapping the red soil of La Rioja for the rich farmland of Castilla-

Leon. Grañón is a typical example of the tiny villages that pepper the trail between Santo Domingo and Belorado. It relies heavily on pilgrim traffic to survive and has little else to see but a church, which in this instance doubles as an albergue. The border between the La Rioja and Castilla regions is actually a short distance outside of the village, but if there was a sign indicating so, neither Rene nor I noticed it. About 90 minutes later, we passed through the village of Viloria de la Rioja, the birthplace of Santo Domingo, not that you would know it. The house in which he was born was demolished in the 1990s, and the font in which he was baptised has been removed from the church. Why a handful of village idiots decided to ignore their most famous son yet keep the word "Rioja" in the town's name is anyone's guess.

Rene and I spent much of the day in deep conversation, mainly because he either could not or would not stop talking. Inevitably the conversation turned to Rene's lofty height, and, God above, did I regret opening that can of worms. Villages came and went as Rene spoke at great length on how miserable it was to be so tall. Simple tasks such as fitting into a plane seat or driving a car were considerable challenges to him, not to mention clothing. He told me how he once walked into a large tailor's shop in Berlin in hopes of finding a suit that would fit him. Taking one look at him, the owner said, "If I had a suit that fits you, I'd sack all my fucking tailors!"

As we entered Belorado, I was running desperately low on convincing ways to nod sympathetically to things I could in no way relate to and was relieved to see a cafe open for business. Hoping that changing the subject to food might cheer Rene up, I suggested we stop for a bite to eat, to which he concurred. As we stepped inside, all heads turned to Rene, necks turned skyward in amazement at such a sight, which gave me some insight into what it must be like for him to be gawped at so often in a day. While Rene was at the bar choosing from the tapas on offer, two old men passed me on their way to the exit, their hands bent at 90-degree angles with their arms stretched high over their heads, eyes wide in apparent disbelief. I can only assume the morons thought I might be completely unaware that the man I came in with was a full head and shoulders taller than me. If I had known the Spanish for "fuck off", I probably would have said it to them.

Unfortunately, my sympathy cup run didn't last long. As soon as our food was brought to us, Rene took a moment to berate me for eating meat with almost militant vegetarianism. Still, I kept company with him because it seemed like nobody else would, and the girls leaving him behind seemed less coincidental now. Changing subjects, Rene lamented how earlier in his Camino, some ne'er do well had stolen his boots, probably as some kind of trophy due to their whacking great size. While this was terrible, I was uncomfortable with how comfortable he was sharing all the intimate details of his life with me, a relative stranger. Whether it be how he was once stabbed with a screwdriver during a stint as a nightclub bouncer or how his girlfriend dumped him over the phone *during* sex with another man — nothing was off the table. While these were traumatic events in this young man's life, his depressing stories were sucking the little joy I had left out of me. As I was about to abandon hope of ever feeling happy again, I remembered a famous quote from English theologian Thomas Fuller, "The darkest hour is just before the dawn". At almost that instant, something remarkable happened. As if a switch was flipped, Rene's frown abruptly turned upside down, and suddenly he was full of vim and vigour. Before I knew it, we were on our feet and out the door, returning briefly because, for some reason, the owner had to remind us to pay for our food. As we left the second time, my wife called to check in with me, and Rene even asked to chat with her for a minute. This had the added benefit of putting her worrying mind to rest, as she now knew I had the BFG as backup should any malfeasance come my way.

What followed was an afternoon of merrymaking around Belorado. With a population of around 2000 people, it is a decent-sized village and, since we had just stopped for lunch, it was not too demanding to explore right away. Belorado's story is one of constant change, with Jews, Christians and Muslims living together in relative peace between the time of original settlement by the Romans followed by King Alfonso 1 of Aragon in 1166 up until the expulsion of the Jews in 1492. Despite a rich history, the relatively-modern 15th-century castle Church of Santa Maria is the oldest still-used building in Belorado, although that is only the nave, with the rest of the building being much newer. Rene and I decided instead to visit the ruins of the Church of San Nicolas to the north of the village, of which all that remains is a stone porch attached to a clock tower.

By now, it was around 6pm, which left the chances of finding space in an albergue slim to none. Since neither of us had the appetite to even try, the two of us (mostly him) decided it would be a good idea to save money and share a hotel room. The hotel of choice was just off the main square of Plaza Mayor and was staffed by a woman who looked like she had one foot in the grave a long time ago. When we asked her for a room and got no response, a much younger woman appeared from around the corner to check us in. Between the frantic wringing of her hands and glances at the clock, she had the look of someone with too much on their plate to care about Little and Large.

However, Rene's odd behaviour was about to make a stunning comeback. After about an hour of verbal diarrhoea, he announced he was ready for the real thing and, without bothering to shut the door, proceeded to rapidly evacuate his bowels in a way that was elephant-like in volume. As I desperately tried to smother myself, he used a heroic amount of toilet paper which, predictably, prevented the toilet from flushing. Mercifully, Rene at least thought fit to pull up his shorts at this point before leaving the room to my fast-dissolving nostrils. To my absolute horror, he returned two minutes later with the nauseated-to-be lady who checked us in, whom he beckoned to view his deposit in all its glory. When she had no idea what he was saying, never mind why he was pointing at his own excrement, Rene pulled the chain, upon which the contents of the toilet disappeared as normal. I sometimes wonder if that poor woman ever talks to her friends or family about the time a colossus wanted her to watch him flush a toilet successfully.

In desperate need of fresh air and a massive drink of any booze I could find, I ventured out alone. As I was walking across the square, a commotion on the far side caught my attention. An apoplectic shopkeeper had come out of his store to remonstrate with some kids playing football directly in front of it and, by the amount of spittle I could see flying angrily from his mouth, I assumed this wasn't the first time he had done so. In apparent response to some lip one of the kids gave back to him, the man completely lost whatever temper he had left, snatching the ball and taking it back into his shop. Dumbfounded, the kids glanced at one another until the smallest in the group summoned enough courage to go in after him. The temptation to find out how this would unfold was too great, and so I made my way over to see the shopkeeper standing behind his counter, ball in hand. The child (who must have been no older than 8 or 9) had his hands out in apparent apology while the middle-aged owner continued the bollocking, his face now turning crimson from the lack of oxygen. If this had been a cartoon, steam would undoubtedly be coming out of his ears by now. Once he had run out of expletives, the shopkeeper hurled the ball over the child's head towards the open door without taking into account the wooden beam that hung down from the ceiling around halfway between the counter and the door. Directly in its flight path, the ball bounced off the beam, onto the counter, smacked the shopkeeper in the face and fell straight into the boy's hands. I listened to the boys howl with laughter as they ran away, in complete confidence that I could have watched that scene a thousand times without it ever becoming unfunny.

I knocked around town aimlessly until running into Valerie and Heike, who were sitting outside a restaurant with a man I instantly recognised. It was Damian, whom I hadn't seen since Puenta La Reina a week earlier. I relayed to them the bizarre day bookended by chickens and a blocked toilet, which elicited mixed reactions. On one side of me, Damian was creased over with laughter, while on the other, Valarie and Heike nodded along in agreement that this was nothing out of the ordinary for Rene. The girls confirmed my suspicions that walking without him was no accident, yet we were in agreement that terrific company can be found in small doses with him. When he was able to compose himself fully, Damian told us about some of the interesting characters he met through his work as a prison officer back in Canada, and the ladies explained how the Camino was just a small part of an around the world trip they had just started. It was getting late for someone who would probably have to sleep with one eye open, so during the next lull in the conversation, I made my excuses and grudgingly made my way back to the hotel. Heike and Valarie invited me to partake in some recreational drug use that evening, but I politely declined, and that was the last I saw them. I did get a message from Heike about 6 months later, telling me how they all crossed the finish line in Santiago together, which I was glad to hear, albeit tinged with some sadness that I wasn't there to see it in person. I returned to the hotel room to find every single light on with Rene bollock-naked asleep on his bed. Preferring death over waking him, I tiptoed around the room like a dressage horse as I turned out all the lights before lying on my own, fully clothed despite the humidity. For the only time in my life, I was somehow able to wish myself to sleep.

In the morning, a combination of beaming sunlight and clumsy packing from Rene stirred me from my slumber. Peering through trembling fingers, I turned to look at Rene's bed to see he had completely unpacked everything from his backpack in an attempt to repack it and, from the frustrated look on his face, I assumed this wasn't his first attempt. With no stomach for putting up with this for another day, I invited Rene to join me for a coffee so I could tell him yesterday was to be our last day walking together in the safety of a public setting. By the time we arrived at the cafe nearby, it was clear Rene was already in the mindset that we were now some sort of double act that was on course to reach Santiago in lockstep. It would have been unfair to allow him to think this, so I flat out told Rene that it was time to say goodbye. While I felt bad for ditching him so abruptly, I made sure to keep my reasoning for doing so in the context of wishing to complete my Camino solo, rather than his rapidly oscillating mood changes. Predictably, he didn't take this polite rejection well, which made me doubly glad that we were in full view of witnesses and that I had all my kit with me. I was on the receiving end of a few choice words but, as of the time of writing, remain unmurdered. As Rene stormed off (probably) back to the room, I made straight for the trail to give his massive strides less chance of catching me up. If I wasn't sick of the sight of the N120 before, I certainly was now, as the trail clings tightly to it for much of the day. Just desserts, perhaps.

15
A LONG AND WINDING ROAD

‖‖

WHEN YOU SPEND six hours a day walking with (for the most part) only your thoughts for company, you develop quite a complicated internal dialogue. I had spent most of this day hitherto reflecting on the people I had become friendly with and felt uneasy with how much I was turning to others to enjoy this experience. The thought that, at the end of each day, I had to say goodbye to people I became friendly with in case I never saw them again was becoming a little depressing, as I now felt I was beginning to depend on other people to walk with, quite the opposite of my reasons for walking in the first place. Now I had to consider the possibility that I was unconsciously using others until they had served their purposes (the irony of how I treated Rene was not lost on me, by the way). Money was also becoming a bit of a problem. Regularly walking with the same people inevitably involved socialising with them, which almost always involved drinking and staying out late. Not only was this having starting to have a negative effect on my body on top of all the walking, but I was spending too much as well and could not complete my Camino as if I was on holiday. Emotionally, I started to feel some ill effects too. I missed my wife terribly and found myself calling her twice this day alone, despite resolving to only do so once a week. As I climbed the Montes de Oca, I felt more unhappy with each step and probably would have thrown the towel in then and there if I could.

Shortly after passing the municipality of Villafranca Montes de Oca, you come across an unassuming fountain known as "La Fuente Mojapán", around which a curious tale is centred. The fountain is known locally to have been used by pilgrims to soften their stale bread to make it more palatable, giving them the necessary sustenance to tackle the difficult (and sometimes dangerous) mountains, and it is this tradition around which a local legend is based. It tells of a group of pilgrims who stayed the night in Villafranca with the intention of taking their bread to the fountain the next morning. However, upon waking, the group discovered one of their number had already left, taking all of their bread with him. Making straight for the fountain, they arrived to find the thief already there and in a desperate state, choking on the stolen bread. When saved by his friends, he explained that when he attempted to soften the bread with the water, the fountain immediately stopped flowing. He explained that when he tried to crush the bread to eat it anyway, it swelled to form a ball in his throat, blocking his airway. Legend has it that, when the friends decided to forgive him in honour of Saint James, water flowed freely from the fountain again. In a 2009 survey of significant places along the Camino, La Fuente Mojapán came in at number 10, no mean feat for a humble water source when you consider the longevity of the Camino Frances alone. Stopping for water is reason enough alone, but the fountain is a pleasant recreational spot where a tired pilgrim can rest before a challenging ascent. And tall tales are always a bonus.

After passing half a dozen contenders for the World's Smallest Village award, my next stopping point of the San Juan de Ortega monastery at last came into view. As you may remember, Saint Dominic was aided in his grand engineering projects by his apprentice, Juan de Ortega, who would follow him into Sainthood. Born Juan Velasquez in 1080, Saint John spent much of his early career helping Saint Dominic in his mission to aid those on pilgrimage to Santiago. When Saint Dominic died in 1109, John went on pilgrimage to the Holy Land and retrieved a relic of Saint Nicholas of Bari while there. On his way back to Spain, John's ship was caught in a severe storm, during which he prayed to Saint Nicholas, promising to continue his work helping pilgrims if he was saved. John was indeed saved from a watery grave and devoted the rest of his life to fulfilling his promise, starting with the clearing of the bandit-ridden Montes de Oca, leading eventually to me having a bed for the night.

It is believed this monastery was John's final project, although judging by the late Romanesque art, most of the construction must have taken place somewhere towards the late 13th century, making it impossible for the structure to have been completed during his lifetime. It is generally agreed that the three apses in the church would have been built by San Juan somewhere between 1115 and 1130, with construction being continued after his death in 1163. The elaborately carved figures depicting scenes from the life of San Juan on his tomb represent the swan song of the Romanesque period in Spain and is well worth a visit and much has been added in the intervening years, such as the Gothic arches along with the Chapel of Saint Nicholas in the 15th century. Originally under the care of Augustine Canons founded by Juan himself, stewardship of San Juan's eventually passed to the Order of Saint Jerome in 1432 until the monastery was disbanded in 1835. In its sixteenth-century heyday, a pharmacy was developed along with the capacity for at least sixteen pilgrims. However, the sanctuary could not withstand the Camino's fall in popularity, leading to the abandonment of the monastery by the mid-nineteenth century.

Since the Camino's resurgence in the 1980s, a purpose-built albergue has been incorporated into the building with a maximum capacity of fifty pilgrims. If you came to the monastery for the architecture, then stay for the Annunciation Capital. Derived from the Latin word "caput", meaning "head", the capital is the topmost part of a column and is usually there to increase the column's capacity to support the weight above it by increasing the surface area. Ornate carvings, particularly in churches, are not uncommon, but this one is particularly worth mentioning. Various scenes related to Christ's birth are depicted, from Gabriel telling Mary she was to bear a son to the announcement of his birth. However, what is most remarkable about this is known as the "Miracle of the Light", an event that only takes place twice a year, during the spring and autumn equinoxes. It is on these occasions that a single ray of light is able to illuminate the Annunciation of the Virgin Mary, a phenomenon that attracts pilgrims from all over the world to the monastery. Unfortunately, I was here at the exact wrong time of year to experience it but was able to appreciate the mix of art and the divine all the same.

Sadly I also arrived at the wrong time to stay there at all, as the hostel had begun some major refurbishments in April, leaving me without a bed for the evening at a time of day I really shouldn't be. With nothing else around other than a bar, I decided that stopping for a beer, however tempting, would be a significant detriment to my ambition of sleeping indoors — but I did it anyway. While there, I observed with amusement a few Korean pilgrims shriek with laughter as their national team were getting their arses handed to them by Algeria at the World Cup. With beer under my belt, I went back to the trail, reaching the next village of Agés after about 45 minutes of poor conditions underfoot. When I reached the village, I decided to seek out a private albergue, hoping it might increase my odds of finding a bunk for the night. It didn't, but with only comfortable double rooms available, I had no option but to treat myself to one. Tired and suddenly starving, I ate and drank at the bar next door like there was no tomorrow before hitting the hay without even bothering to undress.

The improved night's rest made a world of difference, as much to my mood as my physical condition. I felt fresh and revitalised and, combined with the much more favourable terrain, looked forward to reaching the bustling metropolis of Burgos. About half an hour's walk from Agés is the town of Atapuerca, home to the famous Archaeological Site of Atapuerca, given the status of World Heritage Site by UNESCO in the year 2000. As with many sites of archaeological importance, this one was discovered quite by accident. While work building a railway line was underway in the Atapuerca mountains, human artefacts were found, leading to an official excavation of the surrounding area led by renowned palaeontologist Francisco Jordá Cerdá in 1964. It was during this excavation that these artefacts, along with human fossils ranging from Bronze Age hunter-gatherers to early modern humans, were also discovered. Excavations in the area have taken place almost continuously since, with the area known as Sima de los Huesos (meaning Pit of Bones) found to contain over 5000 human skeletal remains from the Middle Pleistocene period dating back over 350,000 years.

After leaving Atapuerca, the trail took me to the top of the Sierra de Atapuerca, from which my near future could be seen stretched out before me. First, I would have to toil through the suburbs of Burgos to reach the city proper, with nothing but the arid conditions of the Meseta waiting for me on the other side. If it hadn't been for that vista, I would have reached Burgos long before realising it, as is often the case with many large Camino cities. I suppose that labouring through industrial estates and suburbs is the price you must pay for the greater amenities available to you in such places. While I was busy daydreaming about my future, something peculiar happened in my present. As Burgos neared, I became an unwitting recipient of what I can only describe as some sort of blessing. Suddenly before me was a man who looked as if he was freshly returned from several years' being stranded on a desert island, holding an ornate figure of Christ on the cross up to the heavens, which he then brought down to eye level, all while praying for my safe arrival in Santiago (I think). Behind him was a van with a sliding door, the kind that they warn children about, which, judging by his appearance, I assumed to be both his means of transport and home. Immediately beside him was one of those folding wallpaper tables, upon which rested a small plate with some change on it beside an enormous coffee dispenser. Fearing being cursed and/or abducted if I didn't leave anything, I hastily tossed a €2 coin onto the plate, for which I received a cup of the world's worst coffee. It was at this point that I leapt back in surprise as the shaman's dog appeared all of a sudden from behind the van, lunging for me. Fortunately for my underwear, the wretched animal was tied up to a five-gallon jug filled with water/urine but, since I didn't exactly trust the rope connecting the two, I got ready to run if necessary. As this farcical scene unfolded, two pilgrims came up the path behind me, curious to see what was going on. It was then I became acquainted with Isaac and Rodrigo, two young Brazilian men attempting to complete the entire Camino Frances in only two weeks. Even I knew this was an incredibly ambitious target, as they would need to average around 37 miles a day to make it to Santiago in time for their flight home. I was averaging just over 20 miles a day and was feeling the effects, but with four heavily-bandaged knees between them, they had it worse. After promising to watch out for each other in Burgos, I left them with the castaway and the fleas assembled into the shape of a dog, confident that I could outrun them if that rope gave out.

As I made my way through the outskirts, I relished the thought of visiting another city more with every step. With a population of around 180,000, Burgos is second only to Pamplona in terms of inhabitants along the Camino, and I hoped the size of the city would give me a more comprehensive selection of goods and services than I had become used to since leaving the latter. Founded by the second count of Castile, Diego Rodriguez Porcelos, in 884 AD, the region in which Burgos can be found has changed hands several times throughout the last two millennia, being held by Celts, Romans, Goths and Berbers, before finally being conquered in the name of Christendom by King Alfonso III in the 9th century. To defend the region by building over old Roman settlements, Alfonso raised several castles, giving the region its name of Castile, meaning *land of castles*. When Porcelos fortified the region into what now resembles the city of Burgos, it fell under the jurisdiction of the King of Leon, eventually becoming independent in 1065. War has come to define Burgos since, whether it be war with the Moors, Navarre or Aragon, the Peninsular War against Napoleon or even the Spanish Civil War. The city's long and tumultuous history is bookended by two military leaders; one a national folk-hero and the other, a brutal dictator. The former was an 11th-century chieftain by the name of Rodrigo Díaz de Vivar, better known as the Spanish national hero, El Cid. The latter, Francisco Franco, would use Burgos as the seat of his military junta at the outset of the Spanish civil war on the 24th of July 1936, becoming infamous General Franco on the 1st of October, ruling Spain with an iron fist until his death in 1975.

As you would expect, the Burgos of today is rich in ecclesiastical points of interest. The first must-see is the cathedral, in which the chapel of the Lord Constable of Castile can be found. The churches of San Esteban, San Gil, San Pedro and San Lorenzo are also well worth a visit if you have the time, but the magnificent Gothic Cathedral is by far the main attraction. Declared a World Heritage Site in 1984, work began on the construction of the cathedral in 1221, which was consecrated by Bishop Maurice in 1260, but wasn't completed until well into the 15th century. As you look around the cathedral, nothing appears to be out of place, something that is remarkable considering the three hundred year period it took to finish. During this time, Burgos enjoyed its golden age, becoming the foremost centre of commerce in the country until Madrid became Spain's national capital in 1561.

I was pleased to enter the cathedral to learn that my pilgrim passport was finally about to pay dividends, giving me a juicy 50% discount on the €7 entry fee, which also included a much-needed map. Tourists enter the cathedral through the south facade, above which Christ in Majesty stands over the 12 apostles, with a statue of Maurice underneath. The most recent addition to the church are the 17th-century portals on the west side of the building, and in the central arcade, eight kings can be found under a statue of the Virgin Mary, suggesting the monarch considered themselves under the authority of God. The central entrance on this side of the cathedral was reserved for royalty. The crucifix-shaped main floor is over 100 metres long and contains three naves that are surrounded by fifteen chapels. Most notable was the transept that forms the "arms" of the crucifix shape, which is where the tomb of El Cid can be found. The 13th-century tomb of Bishop Maurice can also be found nearby in the centre of the choir.

As I swapped the musty air of the cathedral for the fresh outside, I heard a voice call out my name. I scanned the mass of people before me, eventually discerning the source to be my favourite white-haired, bespectacled German, Bernard. As we approached one another, the first thing I noticed about Bernard was that he was wearing the same flip-flops I had seen him wear each time I was in his company. Now on those occasions, he was stationary, and I never for a moment thought he would actually walk the Camino in something more suited to the beach.

Still, he confirmed as much after we had dispensed with the pleasantries to both my awe and revulsion. Bernard had just arrived in Burgos yet had booked a hotel room in advance in anticipation of the city's main festival of the year, San Pedro y Pablo, which was about a week away. This certainly explained the large crowds of non-pilgrims, and I now lamented going straight to the cathedral instead of grabbing one of Burgos' fast disappearing rooms. I took Bernard's advice and followed him to his hotel to see if there were any rooms free and, much to my surprise, there were plenty. However, at €60, it wasn't the cheapest, but at least the central location made it more palatable. With three days in a row staying in comparative luxury, this decadence was going to be a hard habit to break, but I took solace in the knowledge that I was telling my money where to go instead of wondering where it went.

Bernard and I had agreed to meet later for dinner, and after a quick change and shower, I headed back out to explore the bits of Burgos that weren't inside a church. As I crossed the Plaza de Santa Maria, I met Isaac and Rodrigo coming in the opposite direction. The good news was that there wasn't a dog bite to be seen. The bad news was that after a valiant effort and despite braces, walking poles and all the ibuprofen in the world, the lads had admitted defeat in reaching Santiago without their knees becoming totally bolloxed. I had just happened upon them as they were looking for the bus station, from where they intended to take a 9-hour bus ride to Santiago to at least see the place before they flew home to Rio. The boys looked genuinely heartbroken as I handed over the map of Burgos I had picked up from the hotel reception with the sincere hope that they would get to attempt this incredible, maddening journey again one day.

Not trusting myself without a map, I took the five-minute walk to the tourist office to find staff that were as cheerful as they were obliging to the pilgrim. As the young lady behind the counter was stamping my pilgrim passport, she suggested I take the "little train" to see as much of Burgos as possible in the short amount of time I had here. Tours costing only €2 were on the hour every hour, giving me enough time to head over there to be on the next one. The pick-up point was at a small restaurant next to the cathedral, outside of which I waited patiently while enjoying the free public WiFi Burgos provides to its visitors. As the train/car (almost identical to the one in St-Jean) came into view, I couldn't help but notice the distinct lack of passengers. Knowing that there were no other stops, I can only assume the driver takes the 45-minute tour at the designated time whether passengers come with him or not. I approached the vehicle as he alighted with my €2 coin extended, which he refused to take, gesturing for me to follow him over to a small office on the other side of the square. Side-by-side, we walked in silence as far as the office door, where I handed him the coin. He put it in one pocket and took a small, yellow ticket out of the other, which he then gave to me, before turning around and walking straight back to the train. Why he, I and the coin had to cross the square to do this is anyone's guess, but to complete the absurd ritual, he still asked to see my ticket when I boarded the train, despite me being the only passenger. Even so, the ride was excellent value for money, and the opportunity to see medieval streets merge seamlessly with bustling shopping malls is one I can't recommend highly enough. The satisfaction of not having to walk to see everything I did only increased when the heavens opened, causing people everywhere to scatter like mice for any shelter they could find. During the downpour, a humorous scene unfolded where I feigned urgency to help a family that had clearly been caught in the rain by surprise onto the covered train for shelter. The father appeared to take this as a genuine invitation, however, and began sprinting after the train, showing his wife and child a clean pair of heels. I have no idea if he was seriously trying to abandon his family to avoid total saturation, but just as he was within reach of the last car, the train sped up, leaving the man behind to explain himself to his nearest and dearest.

As we were nearing the drop-off, the rain abruptly stopped, giving way to a fresh spring-like feel in the air. I dashed back to the room to get changed before heading back to the cathedral to meet Bernard, or so I thought. We had informally agreed to meet at 7.30, yet here I was at 7.40 to find the immediate vicinity Bernard-free. After hanging around for a few minutes to no avail, I assumed he had wandered off, so I did the same in search of a meal. The restaurant outside of which I caught the train/bus seemed as good a choice as any, and I was soon stuffing my face happily. After dinner, I decided to go back to the side of the square I was heading towards before I was distracted helping Isaac and Rodrigo find the bus station. I glanced in the first bar I passed to see Bernard engrossed in that night's World Cup fixture, completely unaware of my presence until I sat down beside him. During the next break in play, he thoroughly explained his policy of waiting 5 minutes beyond a scheduled audience before you are essentially dead to him. I wasn't offended, and a pleasant few drinks while watching some decent football followed. The final whistle to end the match was a suitable metaphor for the two of us as we were about to separate, not just for the evening, but for life, as Bernard had decided to stay in Burgos for a few more days. I couldn't blame him — the city was breathtaking, and one afternoon of exploration does not do it justice.

I went back to my room to enjoy what was surely going to be my last night of comfort for the next week or so, for in the morning I was to take on the infamous "Meseta" — the middle section of the Camino Frances between Burgos and Astorga that is characterised by long sections of flat, straight earthen tracks (known as autopistas) that run parallel to the road. Featureless panoramas were what awaited me, often with no shade from the searing heat of the Spanish sun. The next morning, I left the hotel and made my way along the River Arlanzón, crossing the bridge to rejoin the trail. In pleasing contrast, the route out of Burgos was much more enjoyable than the walk in. Far less built-up but still with a few chances to pick up last-minute supplies before the next major city of Leon, at least one week's walk away. I made my way through the oven-like heat, ensuring I collected fresh drinking water whether I was thirsty or not, as there were no guarantees I would come across any for the rest of the day. Anticipating a dull few days coming up, I downloaded an audiobook and bought some cheap earphones on my way out of town, apprehensive about what was to come.

16
MESETA OR BUST

WITHIN A COUPLE of days of leaving Burgos, I couldn't decide whether pilgrims chose to walk the Meseta because of the monotony or in spite of it. I can understand why many are tempted to skip this section altogether, with the excellent public transport links between Burgos and Astorga making it painless to do so. I also noticed that the wonderfully refreshing water fountains that made the Camino possible were also becoming conspicuous by their absence with every step. With nothing but horizon to look at for hours at a time when every exposed bit of skin was prime real estate for mosquitoes, inspiration eluded me, and I could certainly appreciate why pilgrims have often blamed this section of the Camino for distorting their perceptions of time and distance like no other. Boredom was an enemy I was not anticipating when preparing for this endeavour and, during the Meseta at least, I never discovered an effective way to combat it. Yet frustration was not going to make a quitter out of me, and I became determined over time to get through the section as quickly as possible by hitting the brinks slightly earlier each day than the one before.

While at no point did I seriously consider giving up and heading home, I was feeling naive for having ever believed walking the Camino would be a non-stop thrill ride of an adventure. The cheap earphones I had bought in Burgos didn't even live to hear the end of the audiobook, leaving me nothing to listen to but the rhythmic plodding of my own feet. As I marched interminably onwards, I felt like I was at a standstill, which seemed a suitable metaphor for how my life was going. My career had been going nowhere fast for more than a few years, and my home life was much the same. My wife and I had been together for 8 years yet hadn't bought a house or raised a family — a situation that must have been confounding for her. These were the kind of thing 'grown-ups' were supposed to be doing, wasn't it? I have always been a somewhat easy-going chap, but maybe that was the problem. Deciding to come on the Camino was probably the most decisive I had ever done, which felt kind of pathetic when I really thought about it. If nothing else, the Meseta had given me the chance to take a long look at my life and where it was going, as well as a much-needed opportunity to organise my thoughts into a coherent collection.

In 1957, in a quote often misappropriated to John Lennon, the writer Allen Saunders said, *"life is what happens to us when we are making other plans."* He was right. For too long, I had been waiting for life to happen to me while it was passing me by. I was almost thirty and felt I had achieved virtually nothing of significance. Much like the road ahead, not much was going to change soon unless I did something about it but, for now, all I could do was keep going.

On the plus side, my body had never been better prepared for such a rigorous walking schedule. Long gone were the blisters, as was the fatigue, no matter the distance covered. Before long, I found myself in a solid routine ideal for the Meseta, preparation for which started in earnest the night before. For instance, a pre-Meseta walking day would be followed by changing and showering in the usual way, before an ill-advised drink or two in a bar, cafe or restaurant. Now, however, with little or nothing else to do in the evenings, I was able to plan appropriately for my walk the next day, giving me a modicum of choice of where to next lay my head. In addition, by leaving earlier than usual in the mornings, not only was pushing on to the next town or village was less of a gamble when it came to securing a bed for the night, it also spared me from walking for too long when the temperature outside was at its hottest.

Food was also an essential factor when it came to preparation. Not one for a big breakfast, I was always sure to carry enough non-perishable snacks without adding too much weight to my bag, which I ate on the move to save time. Despite my whinging, the Meseta was never so desolate as to leave one without at least a shop or bar, many of which I imagine to be the economic lifeblood of such modest communities. Dealing with the heat was probably the most crucial task of all, for which I had a two-pronged attack. Firstly, I dedicated myself to making certain my water supply never fell below 1 litre, something that is difficult but not impossible. Secondly, I dressed myself each morning in multiple, thin layers that could be removed as cool mornings made way for sweltering afternoons. In addition, I would keep the minimum amount of skin exposed to the sun as possible by wearing long sleeves and trousers at all times. This was partly because shorts and t-shirts would make little difference to comfort levels and partly because I couldn't be arsed emptying a bottle of suncream on myself every day.

Now, as I mentioned earlier, most of the pilgrims I met credited mainstream media, in whichever form, for providing them with at least a basic understanding of what it meant to take on this challenge. However, much like every other topic, the Camino is not immune from know-it-alls, and the Meseta led me to the probably worst I have ever encountered. One evening, they were my bunkmate and came in the form of an obnoxious American with a name I can't remember, so let's just call him Wayne Kerr. He was a gormless sort, by which I mean he was a cringeworthy, lying shit-stirrer. Sharp as a marble, Wayne considered himself a member of an exclusive group of 'real pilgrims' who shunned world comforts while on Camino and I can only assume he used titanium walking poles and wore gel insoles out of irony. When I mentioned that I was considering ending my Camino in Finisterre, he scoffed, insisting the true end to The Way was Muxía. When pressed on his reasoning by other pilgrims, all Wayne asserted confidently, "That's where Martin Sheen goes in the movie". It wasn't long until I felt as if I had little choice but to suggest his mother was a woman of ill-repute and challenge him to join me outside for a bout of fisticuffs. Of course, that scenario existed only in my head and, without the necessary patience or crayons to correct him, I opted to stare vacantly at the unnaturally large space between his eyes, something I am almost sure he took as agreement. May he one day fall over with both hands in his pockets.

While it is true to say I would have been irked if anyone had accused me of walking the Camino solely because I saw it in a movie (and not just because I actually saw it in a TV show first), it would be doubly so now because I would be sharing a cohort with this cretin. Having now officially had enough, I rose to my feet and directed them to take me anywhere as long as it was away from Wayne but, with nowhere else to go, it wasn't long before I begrudgingly hit the hay. My mood wasn't helped by the fact that my fellow guests that night were surely professional snorers with an allergy to bathing. However, I was still able to distract myself. Amusingly, above my head on the wall was a no smoking sign that was almost illegible because so many cigarettes had been stubbed out on it.

Without wishing to sound disrespectful, plenty of villages throughout the Meseta are little to write home about. Few had populations in triple digits, with Villarmentero de Campos registering just 16 residents in the

2004 Spanish census. In most cases, just a single road and a church in varying degrees of ruin (either Romanesque, Gothic or a combination of Romanesque and Gothic) were all one would see. After miles and miles of nothing, lone buildings would appear like oases in a desert of farmland and dust, with one such place being San Bol. San Bol isn't a town or a village, and it is quite simply a single hostel that stands in the middle of nowhere. A municipal hostel without a municipality, a village without any villagers. With the door locked and not a soul to be seen, a few strides was all it took to leave this 'town' behind me.

The first significant place of interest on the Meseta is Castrojeriz. This comparatively large village punches above its weight in terms of heritage, with several churches and a ruined castle steeped in its own history. After the usual 2000-year-old game of hot potato between Celts, Romans, Goths, Moors and Christians, Castrojeriz received a town charter in 974 AD, thought to be the first-ever granted in Castile. Several centuries of prosperity followed for the village until the Revolt of the Comuneros against Holy Roman Emperor Charles V in 1521 led to a steady decline. At the foot of the hill on which the castle ruins stand, the Collegiate Church of Santa Maria del Manzano can be found. It is here that Saint James himself is said to have had a vision of the Virgin Mary, after which his horse left hoofprints that can still supposedly be seen today. Other ruins belonging to the ancient monastery of San Anton can be found just outside Castrojeriz. Built atop what was once the palace of King Pedro the Cruel of Castile, the monastery was run by the Hospital Brothers of Saint Anthony as a place where sick pilgrims on Camino could be cared for. The Brothers specialised in treating a disease characterised by a raised, bright red rash that came to be known as St. Anthony's Fire, a condition that today is a relatively common bacterial infection known as Erysipelas.

Shortly after leaving Castrojeriz, you will encounter an albergue like no other, the Ermita de San Nicolás. Built in the 13th century, it has been taking care of pilgrims ever since in the form of a foot-washing ritual within its tranquil environment. A welcome break from the arid, mosquito-infested conditions of the Meseta, San Nicolás is not an easy place to find refuge in since a maximum of ten pilgrims can be afforded a bed for the night but, after setting off early that morning, I was now able to count myself among them. If I hadn't noticed the small group of pilgrims queueing up outside, I could have easily walked straight past, but I instead stood with them, chatting idly for about an hour before the opening of the hostel at 3pm. As we waited, a hospitalero emerged to give each of us a much-appreciated cup of coffee before standing out on the trail to do the same for passing pilgrims.

San Nicolas de Puentelitero Hospital de Peregrinos reads the sign beside the garden in which I could see wild lavender growing before a backdrop of amber coloured fields. The building itself was more of a stand out feature due to its long, almost shoebox shape, standing magnificently against the bright blue sky, behind which a more modern structure perched, containing shower and washing facilities. The albergue is close to the river Pisuerga that forms the natural border between the provinces of Burgos and Palencia and, much like San Bol, does not belong to any village or town, although it is continually staffed.

The small number admitted as overnight guests on a first-come-first-served basis inevitably results in many pilgrims being turned away. As with many other albergues, boots must be removed and lined up neatly before a foot is set inside. After this, it is time to hand over the pilgrim passport to receive the stamp before choosing your bunk bed for the evening. While choosing one, I looked around and counted only four bunk beds, meaning two of us would have to draw the short straw and sleep on painfully thin-looking mats due to there being no way of configuring the beds in a way that would make room enough for another. A long dining table was set up at the other end of the building, presumably for that evening's meal. While the other pilgrims took time to socialise and familiarise themselves with their surroundings, I wanted to take advantage of the superb washing facilities to give my clothes the maximum amount of time to dry in the baking heat of the Spanish sun. After completing my chores for the day, I joined my fellow pilgrims lying on the grass under the shade of an oak tree in the garden. Although I doubted it would have been permitted, a tinge of regret came over me as I lamented not having the means to camp there and then. I am no expert, but I suspect the conditions for an enjoyable night sleep were likely as close to perfect as possible. Later in the afternoon, we were informed that dinner would be served promptly at 8 but, just beforehand, we were led to an altar and invited to sit down. Our feet were then washed using a large wooden bowl by a middle-aged Italian hospitalero, who then kissed them. When all pilgrims had received the ritual, we joined hands briefly then made our way to the dinner table to eat together by candlelight.

In the morning, we were woken early by tender choral music before being served a rustic breakfast to set us on our way back to the Camino and the unforgiving Meseta. So used was I to tiny, dust-blown outposts that Carrión de los Condes, with its population of over 2000, felt like Gotham City by comparison. Carrión is probably most famous for the Monastery of San Zoilo, which was built in the 10th century in the name of John the Baptist only to be renamed in the 11th century after relics of San Zoilo were brought there. Part of the monastery has been turned into a hotel, and the chance to stay there was one I wasn't about to pass up. As part of the price of a room in what was once the monks living quarters, guests are given free access to the rest of the monastery, including the plateresque cloister containing Renaissance books, manuscripts and over 200 arch keystones. As if that wasn't enough, the fantastic beer garden with a resident pizza oven had me head over heels for the place.

Just a day's walk from Carrión is the town of Sahagún. Sahagún is generally agreed to be the halfway point of the French Way and the point where the lesser-known Camino Madrid merges with that of the Frances. As with many towns of the region, Sahagún's glory days are long gone. Still a noteworthy point on the Camino Frances, the original settlement of the area centred around the Benedictine monastery built in veneration of the 4th-century martyrs Facundus and Primitivus, reaching its apex during the reign of Alfonso VI in the 11th century. Sahagún's development in the centuries that followed was heavily influenced by those Muslims who remained in the area after it was conquered by Christians (becoming known as the Mudejar) and contains some of the earliest examples of this Mudejar architecture, which is instantly recognisable by its intricate, geometric patterns.

It is possible to purchase a Halfway Compostela from the Sanctuary of the Virgin Pilgrim, a refurbished convent and museum just outside of Sahagún, but nothing about such a document appealed to me even though I daresay they are a great deal rarer than a full Compostela. As one leaves Sahagún by crossing the Puente de Canto (The Singing Bridge), they will find themselves in a grove of poplar trees known as Charlemagne's Field of Lances. The section of the Codex Calixtinus known as the Turpin Chronicle tells the story of Charlemagne chasing the Saracen caliph, Aigoland, over the River Cea as follows.

> They caught Aigoland in a region called Campos, next to
> the River Cea, in some meadows of a flat fertile plain. Later,
> by order of Charlemagne and with his help, the excellent
> large basilica of the martyred Saints Facundo and Primitivo
> was erected there. Then the night before the battle, some
> Christians, carefully preparing their arms for the fight the next
> day, stuck their lances into the ground, straight up, in front of

the camp. At dawn, those men who were to receive the palms
of martyrdom for their faith in God found that their lances had
grown bark and were covered by leafy branches. Astonished
beyond telling and attributing the miracle to God's divine
power, they cut them off at ground level. From the staves
whose roots remained buried was born the great forest that
can be seen in that place even today.

Those of Charlemagne's forces wishing for martyrdom in battle with the Saracens were almost certainly granted it, with over 40,000 supposedly perishing in action the next day. In reality, the idea that Charlemagne was defending the pilgrimage route to Santiago does not hold up to even basic scrutiny when you consider the battle allegedly took place around a century before Saint James' remains were even discovered, but remains a good story nonetheless.

Two days after the Singing Bridge, I was in Leon, the unofficial capital of the Meseta and the beginning of the end of the section. Much like Burgos, Leon was one of the largest cities I had ever set foot in that I had previously never heard of. On paper, there were other similarities between it and Burgos. Their populations are comparable, both have a cathedral and are the capitals of their respective provinces with which they share names. Although parallels exist with Burgos in most ways, the approach didn't feel anywhere near as laborious in this instance. It was on this approach that I felt the first drops of rain on my head in what felt like a lifetime ago, a refreshing sensation albeit one tinged with a little homesickness for the British crap, yet familiar, weather. It was probably for this reason that I felt myself drawn to a restaurant called *Albany* later that afternoon, as that was the name of the road I was living on at the time, albeit with considerably less dogshit here. On my waiter's recommendation, I ate a type of cured, smoked meat called cecina alongside a bowl of delicious garlic soup. Located on the banks of the Bernesga River, about two-thirds along the Camino Frances, the 36 districts of Leon boasted an embarrassment of stunning Gothic art and architecture, including the Romanesque 10th-century Basilica of San Isidoro and the cathedral of Santa María de León. It also had a Domino's Pizza, which I'm sure you will agree is just as cool.

If nothing else, Leon appeared to be a success story in blending the old and the new. On the same day, one could join the many tourists by taking a trip to see the city's 1st-century Roman wall before heading to its bustling train station or nearby international airport via its vibrant bus network. Founded under Roman rule as a garrison during the final stages in the conquering of Hispania, Leon eventually evolved into a settled military camp by 74 AD, rising to become the capital of the Kingdom of Leon by 910 AD. Henceforth, the city became pivotal in the fight to reclaim land taken by the Moors during the expansion of Christian kingdoms throughout the Iberian Peninsula between the 8th and 15th centuries. Leon can boast having the first parliament in European history, which was established as part of the Kingdom of Leon that would go on to lose its independence after unification with the Kingdom of Castille in the early 14th century amid widespread prosperity. The late 19th to early 20th centuries saw Leon's urban areas grow dramatically when the coal industry's expansion coincided with the advent of the railroads. By 1983, Castille and Leon resumed political ties in a peaceful movement towards autonomy for the region to include Zamora and Salamanca, which has recently included an attempt to revive its regional language of Leonese.

As my meat and soup digested, I took the two-minute walk to the cathedral to find it astonishingly well preserved, considering almost all of it was built between 1205 and 1301, with the exceptions being the north and south towers that were completed in the 14th and 15th centuries respectively. However, it is the stained glass for which the cathedral is best known. It contains over 1700 square metres within the original windows, making it one of the most substantial bodies of medieval stained glass in Europe. The Cathedral Museum contains nearly 1500 paintings, sculptures and manuscripts ranging from Prehistoric times to Neoclassical. The foundations of the building sit on the original site of a Roman bathhouse to serve the local garrison, briefly becoming the site of a royal palace for Ordoño II of Leon, before finally being converted into a cathedral, in which the King's tomb can be found. The cathedral in front of which I stood is actually the third incarnation. The first fell victim to Moorish raids early in the 11th century, giving way to a much grander design containing three naves, with consecration occurring on the 10th of November 1073 during the reign of Alfonso IX. The third and final Gothic-style cathedral was completed and consecrated by Bishop Gonzalo Osorio in 1302 and has been modified and restored countless times since.

The next contender for your spare time in Leon is only a five-minute walk away — the Basílica de San Isidoro de León, where the tomb of the saint and former archbishop of Seville can be found alongside kings and queens. It was here in 1188 that the inaugural Cortes of Leon took place, giving Europe its first taste of contemporary parliamentarianism. Faced with the possibility of attack from the neighbouring kingdoms of Castile and Portugal, King Alfonso IX called a meeting of his court composed of nobles and clergy and the urban middle class from the cities to discuss the crisis. The Cortes would thereafter mainly deal with property disputes and rule on matters such as whether or not to support the King in declaring war.

Football fans might be interested to learn that I caught bits and pieces of the World Cup in Brazil while in the Meseta, but it was when I crossed the Orbigo river at Hospital de Orbigo that I found myself at the site of its medieval equivalent — The Tournament of 1434. Driven by a lover's rejection, a young Leonese knight named Suero de Quiñones challenged anyone wishing to cross the bridge to first compete in a jousting tournament set to take place between the 11th of July and the 9th of August. Whether Quiñones realised that 1434 was a holy year, meaning pilgrim numbers were higher than usual, is unknown. However, what is known is that there was no shortage of competitors, with Quiñones declaring victories numbering in the hundreds. Facing no such challenge, I put my head down and reached Astorga, and the end of the Meseta, three hours later.

Making my way toward the overcast Astorga sky that signified the end of the Meseta brought with it an intense satisfaction. Yes, it may have had tedium to spare, but it was also vibrant and compelling and, now it was finally behind me, I felt like it had taken me to a better place both physically and psychologically, and will remain forever thankful for the much-needed opportunity for self-reflection. The Meseta is, in a sense, a Camino within a Camino. It is as entertaining and irksome as every other section and just as deserving of your footprints, and I daresay the loudest voices shouting reasons not to walk it come from those who never have. Ready to take on the remainder of the Camino with renewed mental stamina, I resolved to enjoy the places I was passing through more since I would almost certainly never have the opportunity to do so again.

17

I'M (NOT) LOVING IT

||||||||||||||||||||||||||||||||||||||||||||||||||||||||||||||||||||||||||||||||||||||||||||||||||

IF YOU ONLY have time to visit one place while in Astorga, let it be the town hall in Plaza Mayor. It is here, high above the square, that you will see two figures in regional dress on either side of the clock striking the bell above it on the hour every hour since 1748. These captivating 30 seconds are the enduring legacy of the people known as Maragatos, and Astorga is located in the region known as *País de los Maragatos*, meaning Country of the Maragatos. Known as the *'pueblos malditos'* (meaning damned people), the Maragatos are an ethnic group of people believed to be descended from the last Moors in Spain around the 10th century and are known for their distinct food, unique traditions and colourful dress. Not to be confused with the Muslims (known as *moriscos*) who assimilated with Catholic Spain's culture after the open practising of Islam was banned in the 16th century, the Maragotos have fought hard to preserve their cultural identity. The Maragato mule drivers found great success between the 16th and 19th centuries, bringing fish from Galicia inland, with meat and crops going the other way until such 'mulerteering' became obsolete with the arrival of the railways. The English 19th-century travel writer Richard Ford made observations about the insularity of the Maragato in his book, *Gatherings From Spain*, describing them as follows,

> *They, like the Jew and gipsy (sic), live exclusively among their*
> *own people, preserving their primeval costume and customs,*
> *and never marrying out of their own tribe.*

More recently, this mistrust of outsiders has softened somewhat, possibly out of necessity due to the dwindling numbers of Maragato amid the pressure of maintaining their way of life in modern times. They are willing to share details about their weddings and food, with many other details such as dress or courting rituals coming from outside observations. The remaining population of the Maragato is spread over 40 or so villages around Astorga and Leon, but numbers of those remaining to live by the old ways have declined sharply over the last century. Stopping short of recognising the Maragato as an ethnic group, attempts have been made by the local government for their cultural identity and tradition to be maintained through tourism.

Emperor Octavian founded the Roman city (known then as Asturica Augusta) in 14 BC and, by 35 AD, Astorga had become the preeminent city in northern Spain as it was the point at which two major Roman roads met — the Via de la Plata to Merida and the Via Traiana to Bordeaux. This made Astorga valuable in not only military terms but also trade, as the roads allowed for easy deployment of forces as well as the transportation of essential commodities such as gold and copper. However, it is another commodity with which the city would later be associated. Astorga is regarded as the birthplace of European chocolate after Spanish Conquistador Hernan Cortes brought chocolate beans back to Spain from modern-day Mexico. The aforementioned Maragato people transporting the chocolate to the rest of Spain and beyond helped its fame spread. Today, Astorga has a chocolate museum, although how it doesn't melt in a Spanish summer, I don't know.

Astorga has long been a friend to the pilgrim, but albergues here were welcoming to the homeless also. As the Camino fell out of favour in the 16th century, Astorga used this time as an opportunity to house vagrants, who often took to the trail to find shelter. While I was bumbling around the town looking for shelter of my own, I ended up at the tourist office of all places, where I met a delightful elderly couple from Florida. Since we never introduced ourselves by name, I hereby assign them the cliché American names of Hank and Martha. I have always enjoyed the company of Americans, so much so I even married one. On purpose. I find them to be wonderfully unabashed people who are never fearful of appearing uninformed on a topic, nor lacking in confidence when they are not, even when pretending. I knew their nationality before either opened their mouth, as Americans are usually the easiest nationality of tourists to identify. If they are wearing jeans, white trainers and a baseball cap, more often than not, they will hail from the great ol' US of A. Hank was wearing his baseball cap backwards as if he was impersonating a teenager, and Martha wore a contented, grandma-like smile that made her look as though she had come to Astorga to take an apple pie out of the oven. After a few minutes of friendly conversation, it was clear to me that Hank and Martha were under-prepared to walk the Camino in a way that was both humorous and concerning. They had both packed all of their belongings into a single suitcase, apparently forgetting that they would have to carry it with them for 500 miles. Not that it would have helped, as all they brought was clothes.

"I never knew you guys had so many hills!" Hank cried out between bites of a Snickers bar. By 'guys', I assumed he meant Europeans, as I doubt that even a blind man on a galloping horse could mistake me for a Spaniard.

"We might have hills," I replied, motioning to Hank's cap, "but I wish we had baseball caps with the peaks on the back. All of ours have them on the front!"

Expecting a laugh, I was instead met with an amused shake of Martha's head.

"Honey, those are the same thing. He just turned his around!" she said as Hank peered over his glasses at me in apparent concern at my ignorance while pulling another Snickers out of his pocket. Considering Hank's chronic nougat deficiency, I was amazed they had made it this far. That was until Martha revealed to me that they had given up on the thought of actually walking almost immediately after their arrival in Pamplona to start their pilgrimage, wisely choosing to travel by train and bus along the route instead. I met them as they were just about to head to Astorga's bus station, having satisfied themselves with that day's exploration.

My next stop was to be Rabanal del Camino, which came with good and bad news. The good news was that it was only 12 miles away. The bad news was that it was entirely uphill — something even the brutal first day didn't have. Even though the distance was comparatively small and the temperature was strikingly low compared to recent days, I wasn't taking any chances, bringing way more snacks and water than needed. The strain of hauling myself up an unending hill was mitigated by the favourable terrain and abundance of shade in the mountains, with plenty of opportunities to stop for breaks (of which I needed many). Rabanal contains some of the best-preserved Maragato architecture in the region and remains popular with many of the 200,000 pilgrims passing through each year. For centuries, the town has been a popular stopping point for pilgrims who, like me, started one day in Astorga, ready to climb Monte Irago the next. With a population of less than a hundred, Rabanal relies heavily on pilgrims buying trinkets or dining in one of its restaurants set within typical Maragato houses.

After entering the village, I passed places of interest left and right. First up were the 18th-century hermitages of the Blessed Christ of the Vera Cruz and San Jose before I came across the Casa de las Cuatro Esquinas, meaning House of the Four Corners. It was here that King Felipe II was supposed to have spent the night while on his own Camino in the 16th century. While I roamed the village, I took a moment to visit the parish church of Our Lady of the Assumption, which once belonged to the Catholic military order known as the Knights Templar, a society of knights dedicated to protecting pilgrims as they made the dangerous crossing of the mountains. Construction on the church began in the 12th century, although only the apse remains from this era, with most of what I was looking at being constructed in the 18th century. At 7pm every night, an evening prayer service known as Vespers is held in Gregorian chant by the resident Benedictine monks.

Rabanal is an excellent place to stay for campers, with a wonderfully kept campsite close to the Ermita de San Jose but, since no tent had come into my possession since my stay at the Ermita de San Nicolas, brick and mortar would have to do. I made my way up the narrow main street for what felt like the millionth time and happened across a delightful little guest house called El Descanso de Gaia (meaning Gaia's rest), where I checked in and greedily sought out the nearest menu. As I joyously ate and drank, I deftly earwigged a conversation on a nearby table during which a man lectured his companions on the Camino ad nauseum, despite his own admission to having never walked it. I should have asked him where I could get a tent at this hour.

The high altitude made for a frigid morning in Rabanal as I climbed what was left of Monte Irago, reaching the village of Foncebadón less than an hour later. The story of this village is a curious one. After thriving during the middle ages due to the Camino, during which time the village received tax exemption in return for setting waymarkers, the Protestant reformation and the Napoleonic Wars of the 16th and 19th centuries respectively led to a reduction in population, which was hastened by the construction of new highways and railroads during the 20th. By the 1970s, almost all of the village's population had left in search of employment in the nearby cities of Ponferrada and Leon, and by the 1990s, Foncebadón had just two permanent residents (if you don't count the rumoured packs of wild dogs), a mother and son. However, the return of pilgrims in recent times has brought about a bit of a resurgence in the village; the church has been restored, and the cafe and hostels that were once ruined buildings now stand again in apparent roaring trade.

A short time later, I reached the top of Monte Irago which, at almost 5000 feet above sea level, is the highest point of the entire Camino Frances and where the Cruz de Ferro stands. It was placed there in the name of Christianity by a 12th-century hermit named Gaucelmo. As the name suggests, it is an iron cross that sits atop a five-metre wooden pole, the base of which is buried under tens of thousands of small stones. It soon became apparent that, much like those sitting upon countless waymarkers so far, pilgrims are supposed to bring stones with them (either from home or somewhere along the Camino) and place them there to symbolise the dropping of a burden or absolution of sin. The idea of dropping a stone in such a way is much older than the Camino, with people as far back as ancient Rome doing so on mountain trails as a way of giving thanks to the Roman god Mercury for their safe passage. Lacking a stone to do so with, I regretted leaving one on that waymarker in the Pyrenees, feeling a little affronted that no one told me I had to bring one beforehand. Needless to say, whatever burden I would have dropped would have to remain with me while I stood on top of everyone else's. The part of the wooden base that was still visible was almost completely covered at the base by various flags of the world, which I assumed were placed there in lieu of pet rocks. Since I didn't have a flag either, I queued up behind a dozen other pilgrims to disobey my own vow to never take a selfie before scarpering.

Just after the Cruz de Ferro on the way down Monte Irago is the village of Manjarín that has stood abandoned since the 12th century — sort of. Although I couldn't see any evidence of one, the village is apparently home to a hostel run by a man named Thomas that is capable of housing over 30 pilgrims. I rolled up to find seven or eight pilgrims milling around while a stray dog went from person to person begging for food. It was here, I paused for a few minutes at a small shrine dedicated to pilgrims where some kind soul had left out half a dozen coffee-filled thermoses and a few packets of biscuits. The coffee was okay, but the biscuit was so unappetising, it would have been tastier to eat a photograph of one. Not that the dog minded, gobbling up mine gratefully.

After a slight rise, you enter the region of El Bierzo, where the trail descends through the village of El Acebo de San Miguel with its houses made from locally-mined slate adorned with wooden balconies. On the way out of the village, I passed a sculpture of a bicycle made out of rebar in memory of German cyclist Heinrich Krause, who died here in 1987. Reports on the cause of death vary — some say it was a heart attack, while others say the death was caused by a fall from the bike at high speed. Whichever it was, the mere thought of facing these steep declines on a bicycle was enough to make me think it could have been both, and his death has been used as an example to warn cyclists of the potential danger they face ever since.

The subsequent villages of Riego de Ambrós and Molinaseca were little more than a blur as I tumbled (literally a couple of times) down the mountain towards my next stop of Ponferrada. The rocky and uneven surface I had covered while ascending and descending the mountain in quick succession via the highest point in the entire Camino had played merry hell with just about every joint below my chin, leaving me exceedingly short-tempered. Skinned knees and swollen ankles aside, I once read somewhere that the vast majority of those who die whilst mountaineering do so on the descent, so I decided to call it a draw between myself and Monte Irago.

Unfortunately for me, Ponferrada is surrounded by mountains, which meant the respite for my failing limbs would only be temporary. With around 70,000 inhabitants, it is second only to Leon in terms of provincial population counts and would be the last significant urban centre I would be visiting before reaching Santiago, and I was intent on making it count. The city is unique in the sense that it is a municipality in its own right, while also the capital of the El Bierzo region, which is contained within the larger province of Leon, itself held within the autonomous community of Castile and Leon. Some of these communities have traditionally been divided into legally defined smaller districts known as *comarcas*, of which El Bierzo is the only one in the region. I felt as if I was the centre of a vast set of Russian dolls just standing there.

After the region was conquered by Augustus Caesar in 25 BC, it soon became the site of the largest gold-mining operation in the entire Roman Empire, evidence of which can still be seen today, such as the UNESCO World Heritage site of Las Médulas. After the Visigoths and Moors had their fill following the fall of the Roman Empire, the town was rebuilt by the so-called "Emperor of Spain", Alfonso III. Ponferrada gets its modern name from the Latin, Pons Ferrata, meaning Iron Bridge, which has nothing to do with the Romans but instead refers to the iron bridge built to help pilgrims cross the river Sil in 1082. By the end of World War I in 1918, the mining industry in Ponferrada was revived, this time in the form of coal, which led to an economic boom that lasted until the mass-closure of coal mines in the 1980s. The era of uncertainty that followed plunged the city into a social and economic upheaval that lasted until the dawn of a new millennium that brought significant commercial investments and infrastructure projects to Ponferrada. Coal production has since made way for wine-making, with commercial vineyards reintroduced to areas for the first time since Roman times, with tourism and agriculture making up the rest of the local economy. Ponferradans (I have no idea if they call themselves that) today are well-known for their love of cycling, with plenty of routes and tracks to enjoy around the city, including the 200 mile long Miranda Circular that encircles the El Bierzo region and the upcoming 2014 UCI Road World Championships that September being hosted here.

Itching to do my bit for Ponferrada's tourism industry, I set my sights on its crown jewel, the 12th century Castillo de los Templarios. When Leonese king Ferdinand II gifted the town to the Knights Templar in 1178 as a reward for defending the faithful while on Camino, they set to work fortifying the city in 1187, with the construction of the castle being completed in 1282. However, the Templars would only have around 30 years to enjoy their creation after a combination of jealousy and distrust for the wealth and power they had accumulated compounded their loss of the Holy Land, leading to Pope Clement V disbanding the order in 1312. Ownership of the castle would be disputed until the marriage of King Ferdinand II of Aragon and Queen Isabella I of Castile in 1469 effectively united Spain, bringing the fortress under control of the crown in 1486. Legend of the Knights Templar in Ponferrada has not diminished in the centuries since, with the order being honoured annually in a town-wide ritual held under the first full moon of the summer in The Night of the Templars. During this event, the Grand Master of the Knights Templar, Fray Guido de Garda, returns to the city to place the Holy Grail and the Ark of the Covenant in the custody of its citizens, who all make their way to the castle in medieval dress.

As I circled the outer perimeter of the castle twice, looking for the entrance, I was able to appreciate how intimidating the fortress must have been for enemy soldiers, let alone a pilgrim who couldn't find his arse with both hands. After finally finding it, I paid a modest admission fee of only €3, which afforded me an enjoyable couple of hours admiring the views of Ponferrada from the ramparts, roaming some of the 172,000 square feet of castle grounds and studying some of the books on display in the particularly engrossing Templum Libri exhibit. Installed as a permanent exhibit in 2010, the library contains over a hundred works donated to the city by local bibliophile Antonio Ovalle Garcia. It is spread over two rooms, covering religious codices and manuscripts in one, with science and humanities in the other. I was particularly interested to see the facsimile of the Book of Kells after seeing the 9th century original in Trinity College, Dublin, just a few months earlier. The display is nothing short of spectacular, and the chance to gain even a small insight into the knowledge and wisdom that those in the medieval period considered most valuable is one I cannot recommend highly enough.

I headed back out into the baking heat and made my way to the town centre, satisfied that I would probably strike a decent compromise between price and comfort level if I started searching for a hotel there. This turned out to be a poor choice as none were forthcoming at any level of either, so I instead settled on finding the tourist office, where I hoped at best to find a recommendation and, at worst, a map. The prophecy served to be self-fulfilling as, despite seeing a sign pointing the way to the tourist office, I still couldn't find it after repeated, thorough searches of the general vicinity in the direction of the pointy end. Then, after a vexing march around the centre of Ponferrada, and in movie cliche style, I found it just as I was about to give up. In a way that was baffling to me, I had outdone myself in navigational incompetence and unwittingly already walked straight past the bloody place, not once, not twice, but thrice. Kicking myself, I pushed the door to find it recently locked, a state in which it would remain for the next 1 hour and 55 minutes.

While I have nobody to blame but myself for missing the closing time by just minutes, Spanish businesses and their opening hours, particularly in larger towns, was an area I was still grappling with. This hadn't been the first time I had found tourist centres impossible to find or closed when I finally did. On many occasions, my arrival in a new town or village coincided with the 'siesta' (a short nap taken in the early afternoon, usually coinciding with the hottest part of the day), a Spanish tradition I was surprised to see still going strong. It was often the case that I would be trying to find a tourist office, only to repeatedly find myself there at the furthest time from its reopening. Given Spain's economic problems over recent years, it was hardly surprising that they weren't open all hours. Throughout the Camino Frances, I found Spanish high streets peppered with closed-down businesses, a situation undoubtedly accelerated by the economic downturn in Europe and the wider world over the previous decade. Anecdotally, I had heard a lot about the plight of young Spaniards struggling to find work. During my time in Spain, I rarely seemed to see people commuting or (unless it was a bar or restaurant) even at work, with most areas of the Camino I passed through appearing to suffer from at least some level of deprivation.

At a loss of what to do next, I bought ice cream from a vending machine and sat on a public bench to consider my next move. Hoping for a brain wave but getting a brain freeze, I stomped towards a nearby office building into which I saw some people (who were most definitely awake) entering. As I stepped through the doors, I stopped in my tracks to bask in the marvellous feeling of air conditioning on my skin. So beguiling was this sensation, it caused me to instantly forget why I went in there, and I stood stock-still in the middle of the reception area as, one by one, pairs of eyes fell upon me before a voice called out, "Hola", jolting me back into reality. It had come from the receptionist, a petite young lady whose eyes were barely visible over the desk from my vantage point. I lumbered up to the desk where we proceeded to have a delightfully hilarious conversation, during which we took turns typing questions and answers into Google translate on her office keyboard. Her name was Isabella, and I have no idea if she was on her lunch break or if part of her job was ferrying lost tourists around but, when she finally understood what I was after, kindly dropped everything to give me a lift to an area of town more suited to my needs. After a short drive, she parked up and drew a crude map of the downtown area of Ponferrada, which helpfully included a few hotels, restaurants and attractions. My gratitude for that map can never be overstated since, while I had studiously learned how to ask for directions in Spanish, it hadn't occurred to me until that moment that I hadn't learned any vocabulary pertaining to possible answers. I had no idea of the English translation for essential words such as left, right, straight, street, road, avenue, corner or roundabout. I am sure that asking for directions to somewhere while nodding along in apparent understanding before striding confidently in the opposite direction was likely perplexing to the locals. After waving Isabella goodbye, I took the short walk to the nearest hotel on her map. Upon arrival, the owner of the establishment sensed how tired and frustrated I was and poured me a beer for my troubles, which was welcome, before sliding over the bill, which wasn't.

I downed it anyway before heading to my room, where I took a quick shower and changed into some new clothes, perking myself up no end. Back down in the hotel reception, I picked up a larger, more detailed map of Ponferrada on which a street name caught my eye, Calle Manchester. I decided that the short walk would be worth the novelty of at least taking a photo of the sign and duly did so, although the street is essentially a lap of an industrial estate that looked like an ideal site for a gangland murder. On my way back to the hotel, I happened across a billboard advising me of my close proximity to a McDonald's restaurant. Partly because I was still a bit homesick, and partly because I hate myself, I decided to seek it out to fulfil a long-held desire to drink a beer inside a McDonald's, something that was not possible at home (for obvious reasons). As usual, my efforts to find the place I was looking for were embarrassingly protracted. When you walk for more than an hour and are still unable to find a giant, illuminated version of the most recognisable symbol in the world, your wayfinding skills are seriously lacking. When I eventually found it, I was in such a poor mood that I didn't even want it anymore, but drank one purely to spite myself.

18

MAY THE ROAD RISE TO MEET YOU

||||||||||||||||||||||||||||||||||||||||||||||||||||||||||||||||||||||||||||||||||||||||||||

I KNEW THAT after Ponferrada, I might have to be dealing in cash for a few days and so took out the maximum amount I was comfortable with carrying in a money belt with a zip broken in a way that made it look as though it was talking as I walked. The trip to the cash machine took me further from The Way than I expected and, as is easily done in the cities, I got a bit turned around while trying to get back on it again, eventually ending up drifting onto the local campus of the University of Leon, where I was delighted to learn they have their own stamp for such occasions. After being pointed in the right direction by a couple of PhD students, I spent the next hour making my way through the suburbs initially built to house the workers drawn to Ponferrada by the coal boom of the 1960s. This sharp growth seemed to have swallowed up several places I was now passing through, such as Columbrianos, a town in its own right that predates Ponferrada by at least a century but now makes up a small part of the municipality of the same name. The history of my own home town of Manchester seemed to parallel that of Ponferrada, as it transformed from an unimportant Lancastrian outpost to a thriving industrial metropolis at the turn of the 19th century thanks to the industrial revolution. In Manchester's case, the explosion of the textile industry caused the rapid urbanisation of the surrounding region now known as Greater Manchester.

As my Camino wore on, I came to appreciate that all the villages and hamlets I was passing through deserved to be considered in their own right, no matter how small or absorbed into larger cities they had become, with their own history and cultural identity. A couple of hours after leaving Ponferrada, I reached one such place, the wine-producing village of Cacabelos. Free from the clutches of Ponferrada but still within the El Bierzo region, Cacabelos is one of the bigger villages along the Camino Frances with nearly five and a half thousand inhabitants and counts itself as one of the province's Galician speaking councils. On the 3rd of January 1809, the Peninsular War and Spanish War of Independence overlapped at the Battle of Cacabelos, which took place at a bridge over the River Cúa on the outskirts of the village. British rearguard troops under the command of Sir John Moore were surprised at the bridge on their way to A Coruña by French cavalry dispatched from Ponferrada. As the British regrouped on one side of the bridge, the French forces, led by Brigadier General Auguste François-Marie de Colbert-Chabanais, did the same on the other. Impatient to press home his advantage, Colbert-Chabanais elected not to await reinforcements and ordered his men to storm the bridge there and then, but they were subsequently mown down by the British rifles waiting for them. Colbert-Chabanais did not live to see the consequences of this blunder himself, with his death coming during the short period between the time his fateful orders were given and the time they were carried out. Hubris caused him to consider himself well out of musket range did not leave room to contemplate the Baker rifle or the man holding it, Thomas Plunket, a marksman confirmed to be able to hit a target from over 650 feet. By the time French infantry support did arrive, the British defensive position was so strong that the momentum the French had enjoyed was well and truly lost, leaving the British free to make their way back to A Coruña unimpeded.

Although there were plenty of accommodation choices in Cacabelos, I still had a bit left in the tank and so decided to keep walking to the next sizable town of Villafranca del Bierzo. With less than a quarter of the Camino Frances remaining, it came as no surprise that places such as Villafranca owe their continued existence to the pilgrims that made their way before me as far back as the 9th century, with Villafranca even being recommended as a resting point in the fabled Codex Calixtinus two centuries later. Ownership of Villafranca bounced between various nobles over the next several hundred years before the town fell victim to various calamities, most notably plague, flooding and the English. From 1820 to 1823, the Liberal Triennium took place in Spain, during which the country was run by a liberal government following a military coup in January 1820 against Ferdinand VII. This period of unrest led to the 1822 territorial division of Spain that rearranged many of Spain's provinces and even created new ones, such as the Province of Villafranca in 1822, of which Villafranca del Bierzo was the capital. However, the new province was to be short-lived, with absolutism being restored in October 1823, repealing the declarations made three years earlier. Although the territorial division of Spain a decade later in 1833 did restore many of the changes made in 1823, the Province of Villafranca was not one of them. Today the village has a population of over five thousand and all the modern conveniences you would expect with more bars, cafes and bars than you can shake a stick at. Finding myself with no stick to shake at anything, I spent a congenial afternoon walking its charming streets and squares.

The landscape and wildlife on the trail to Santiago are as spectacular as they are varied and can be enjoyed right from the off — beginning with the thick forested French side of the Pyrenees, to the hot and humid Spanish side and on to rich Basque farmland. I was delightfully surprised that so much of the initial part of the route remained unspoilt, leaving native wildflowers such as the Pyrenean Eryngium, Angelica and Scabious to be enjoyed. If you are a more knowledgeable botanist than me (you are, trust me), you could probably expect to also spot Trumpet and Short-leaved Gentians, Alpine Bird's-foot Trefoil, Green and Stinking Hellebore, Hepatica, Viper's Bugloss, Cut-leaved Mallow, Meadow Saffron, Merendera, Grass-of-Parnassus, Hoary Mullein and even Wood Scabious later in the summer. Naturally, where you find interesting flora, fauna won't be far. These botanical riches attract butterflies like the Purple-shot Copper, Wall Brown, Camberwell Beauty and Clouded Yellow. Those of an ornithological leaning may be interested in some of the birdlife active in the region including the Rock Bunting, Black Redstart, Short-toed Treecreeper and Golden Orioles, to name but a few. I later learned of a hide (sadly, away from the route) near Santa Cilia where Griffon Vultures can be seen coming to a muladar — a traditional enclosure where dead animals are left out to be devoured. Further along the Camino trail, more roadside plants wait to be discovered, such as the Fumana Ericoides and the pink rock rose, with birdlife becoming more varied in the form of the Red-billed Chough, Melodious Warbler, Blackcap and Black Woodpecker.

What interested me most about Villafranca was its natural heritage. The surrounding area contains incredibly diverse species and ecosystems in a relatively small space, geographically speaking. This is primarily due to the overlapping biogeographic regions of the warm, dry Mediterranean, characterised by tree species such as the Holly and Cork Oak and the Eurosiberian, bringing beech, oak, birch, and fir trees to the table. For nature lovers, this was paradise and, if there was ever an argument that the modern human can live harmoniously among nature, this was it. To my eyes, the area pleasantly appeared unaltered by the humans who make use of places such as the cork groves, taking no more than they need, as farmers and nature-lovers traverse the nexus of paths that link pastures, meadows and orchards, lined by trees that have seen them come and go all the while. Humid forests overflowing with ash and poplar trees provide shelter for the vast array of fauna in the region, from the wolf to the lizard fed by the Burbia River. It is hard to imagine a place so tranquil is most famous for being the site of a battle that took place in the year 791 AD between Christian rebels from the Kingdom of Asturias and the Emirate of Cordoba for control of the Iberian peninsula.

Back to the topic of trees, Villafranca's pièce de résistance is, without doubt, the Cypress Tree of the Annunciated (I have no idea if it should be capitalised, but it sounds grand enough to warrant it), which can be found standing next to the Convent of the Annunciation. Originally the site of a pilgrim hostel, the convent was founded by the Marquis of Villafranca in 1606 when his daughter declined an arranged marriage to take her vows as a nun. Just 13 years later, in 1619, the tree was planted to commemorate the arrival of Saint Lawrence of Brindisi's remains, making it the oldest tree of its type in Spain and, at over 100 feet tall, the tallest too. At just over 400 years old, the tree is a mere infant compared to the most aged known cypress, a bald cypress tree on the banks of the Black River in the US state of Louisiana that was found to be over 2,624 years old in 2018. However, its (relatively) short life presiding over the monastery has not been without its challenges, with the tree being found to be riddled with pests when it was tested in 2001, three of which are apparently incurable. Despite feeling a damn sight better than the tree probably was, I was still interested to learn about a quirky feature in the nearby Church of Santiago the Apostle that occurs nowhere else in the entire Camino. In the event that a pilgrim is too injured or sick to complete their Camino by the time they reach the church, they are still permitted to receive the same graces they would have if they had made it all the way to Santiago. That is provided one has covered the necessary distance, confessed one's sins, received holy communion, prayed for the intentions of the church and, perhaps most bizarrely, entered the church using the north entrance known as the "door of forgiveness". Bloody terms and conditions.

I rose to face my final day not only in Villafranca but in the province of Leon, which I would leave for Galicia before the day was out. The walk out of Villafranca begins with a choice between two ways of getting to the same place. One involves a gentle yet dull walk along the main road through the Valcare valley, and the other, a brutal 1300 foot climb over it. It was time to decide whether to prioritise my eyes or my thighs. I opted for the former for two reasons. Firstly, I very much doubt that anyone in history has been glad that they walked along a busy highway. In fact, although it didn't seem so to me, the most common bugbear that I heard from other pilgrims was the excessive amount of roadside walking involved. Secondly, the climb, although difficult, would at least be over relatively quickly, leaving me to lord it over the pilgrims below as I enjoy the view of them, twirling gaily amid the stunning scenery like a sweaty Maria von Trapp. When I reached the apex, the reality was far less merry, with the trail virtually throwing me up into the cloud-filled sky to see 10km of nothing in particular before dumping my weary legs back down in what looked like the Spanish version of Royston Vasey.

The next couple of hours were thankfully mishap-free. As I made my way up towards my next stopping point of O Cebreiro, I passed through a hamlet containing a small cluster of houses called Las Herrerías. It was here I passed a stable where a local entrepreneur had set up what resembled a taxi rank, with four horses taking the place of the black cabs. For a fee of €40, one could be carried up the valley to O Cebriero, sparing the body another steep climb. A man tending to the horse at the front gave me a brief, half-hearted pitch in three different languages to which I gently shook my head. I have ridden horses before, but this sounded like an indulgence too far at the expense of an animal. So off I went, using all of my agility to avoid stepping in the evidence of previous trips along the narrow path. It didn't take long for me to recognise why the horse owner chose to set up shop where he had. The 20km I had walked until that point had yielded a net elevation increase of around 200 metres, yet the next 10km would see an increase of over 600 metres. The incline was becoming so steep that I thought I would be upside down by the time I crossed into Galicia. When I did cross the border on all fours approximately two months later, a stone marker gave the distance to Santiago as a discouraging 152km. A whispered "Bastard" was all I could muster at the sight of it, as I waddled still further uphill towards the lush, green pastures of O Cebreiro, desperately fighting an impending spell of ugly man-crying. I should have just paid the €40.

Established in the middle of the 9th century, O Cebreiro is home to the church of Santa Maria la Real, the only pre-Romanesque church that remains intact on the whole of the Camino Frances, where one can get a close-up look at one of the two holy grails. Now you might be thinking, as I was, since when were there two holy grails? I have seen *Indiana Jones and the Last Crusade* and distinctly remember Jones and the Nazis vying for possession of a single Grail. It certainly would have been a much shorter movie if Jones and the Nazis could have had one each. In the interest of full disclosure, no credible source has ever claimed that the Holy Grail in O Cebreiro is the same one used by Christ at the Last Supper, but is instead one that was used by the parish priest sometime in the 14th century where it is claimed the bread and wine turned into actual flesh and blood, a claim that was certified as the Miracle of O Cebreiro by Pope Innocent VIII a century later. The story behind the miracle tells of a peasant named Juan Santin from the nearby village of Barxamaior, who made his way to receive the Eucharist at Santa Maria despite a bitter snowstorm sweeping the area. Upon entering the church, the peasant was mocked by the priest (of all people) for being the only person willing to risk their life for mere bread and wine in such treacherous conditions. However, the priest was soon about to eat his words instead because, when he looked down, the bread and wine had inexplicably turned into flesh and blood. How awkward for him. I was interested to learn that in 2015, two historians called Margarita Torres Sevilla and José Miguel Ortega del Río published a book called *Kings of the Grail*, in which they claim to have found the true grail in the same Basilica of San Isidoro in Leon that I had visited just a week before arriving in O Cebreiro. Of course, since I was there in 2014, I couldn't have known that I had the opportunity to lay my eyes upon arguably the most significant religious artefact in human history but felt miffed nonetheless. It might be the sour grapes talking, but, in my opinion, this second "Holy Grail" is well-deserving of those air quotes I just did.

Built by the Celts that populated the area more than 1500 years ago, O Cebreiro is perhaps best known for the stone roundhouses with thatched roofs called *pallozas* that are dotted around the village, a few of which have been kept as an ethnographic museum to the way of life that existed until as recently as the 1960s. Visitors to the pallozas are treated to a recreation of how the townsfolk would have lived in these dwellings, where entire families would sleep on beds that surrounded a fire, with livestock in a room below them and curing meat in the rafters above. Examples of such habitations are representative of other places in Europe to which the Celts made their way, such as Scotland or Ireland and the design of low, rounded walls and aerodynamic straw roofs are a simple yet ingenious way to keep cold air out and warm air in. To my mind, the pallozas brought images I associated with the cottages my grandmother would describe from her youth in Ireland and the glorious views contrasted with the miserable weather certainly felt like the summers I used to enjoy as a child. All that was missing was the heady aroma that can only come from a turf fire, and I stepped into one of the handful of pubs, half expecting to see one. Finding none, the bowl of soup and glass of red wine in the cosy atmosphere soon chased away the disappointment. As I ate and drank, I felt an unspoken connection with these people in a way I hadn't at any point on the Camino so far. Perhaps my Irish heritage helped me identify with these people who were just as protective of their culture, history and language with a simple way of life tied closely to nature.

At times in Galicia, it felt eerie, perhaps even post-apocalyptic, as if I had the whole country to myself, with the faces of non-pilgrims becoming few and far between. It wasn't my imagination — a dearth of opportunities has seen the region's youth leave for larger cities in their droves, a problem that has spread throughout the country, referred to as 'España Vacía' meaning 'Empty Spain'. I was shocked to learn later that entire Spanish villages can be bought for less than the price of a 1 bedroom flat in London due to their total abandonment, such as the hamlet of Xerdiz, about 90 minutes drive from Santiago and just five minutes from the nearest beach, where that £400,000 burning a hole in your pocket would get you six large properties and still leave you enough change to fully renovate before buying friends to live in them.

19

DON'T FEAR THE REAPER

GRANDAS DE SALIME is a small town about 140km north of Ponferrada and was once home to a man named Miguel Ángel Muñoz Blas. On the 11th of September 2015, the 39-year-old sat in a police station after being arrested for the murder of missing American pilgrim, Denise Thiem. In calm yet chilling testimony, he described in detail how he lured the 41-year-old to his property and killed her with a blow to the head before removing her hands and burying her body. Now I know what you must be thinking. This book about self-discovery or whatever just took somewhat of a dark turn, but I would be remiss if I didn't remind anyone thinking about walking the Camino that, just like anywhere else, The Way can be a microcosm of the rest of the world, wherein you will find the best and worst of humanity. Now, for those pilgrims who are on the wrong end of the latter, chances are it will range from the minor annoyance of having something stolen to a disconcerting turn of verbal abuse. However, this was not to be the case for Denise Thiem, who sadly found herself in the right place, but at the wrong time.

Muñoz used his own painted yellow arrows that were made to resemble the genuine Santiago-facing ones to misdirect Denise away from the trail towards his home in Castrillo de los Polvazares, where he lay in wait. Thiem was not the first to fall for this trick, and a handful of pilgrims have since come forward to report encountering Muñoz after making the same mistake. These previous 'attempts' at luring pilgrims ultimately proved to be Muñoz' undoing, eventually leading police to consider him a suspect and, despite keeping him under close surveillance in the hopes he might unknowingly reveal to them the location of the body, he never did. The murderer didn't do himself any favours in avoiding suspicion after exchanging $1000 (US) just one day after Thiem was last seen alive in Astorga — something that would have been highly unusual for a man living in rural Spain.

As for motive, no one can be sure, and Muñoz himself has revealed nothing. Sexual seems the most likely, and the removal of the hands suggests he wanted to hide the identity of his victim in case the body was eventually discovered. Despite numerous appeals from Thiem's family and the extensive application of the FBI and Spanish police resources used to find her, all came to nought. Even US Senator for Thiem's home state of Arizona and former presidential hopeful John McCain became involved, raising her case with Spain's Prime Minister, Mariano Rajoy, for help in the search to no avail. After his eventual arrest at a bar over a hundred miles away, Muñoz led police to a wooden shack on a nearby farm, where locals had said the 'recluse' had been living since he moved there from Madrid in 2011. Despite their investigation, Spanish police would later admit that without Muñoz's eventual confession to the crime or his revealing of the location of the remains, it would have been improbable that the case would ever have been solved.

Based on her lack of social media updates, it was determined that Thiem went missing on or shortly after the 4th of April. Her brother,

Cedric, became concerned after not talking with his sister via Skype for several days as they had never failed to reach out to one another since Denise began her round-the-world trip. After becoming dissatisfied with the response (or lack thereof) from Spanish and American authorities, Cedric eventually travelled to Santiago himself on the 20th of April to submit a missing person's report before walking the Camino backwards from the finish line of Santiago to the point in Astorga where his sister was last seen alive in the slim hopes of running across her on the trail. With over a third of the Camino's total distance to cover before reaching Astorga, he eventually decided to go straight there, focussing on the last place his sister was seen alive by canvassing local citizens and police — but it was all in vain. Several other women did come forward due to the publicity Cedric's investigation was causing to reveal being harassed by men on the route, further leading him to believe that foul play was involved in his sister's disappearance.

More foreboding to Cedric was his discovery of the attempted abduction of a female jogger shortly after his sister's disappearance. The 50-year-old woman was approached by two men whose faces were partially covered in a car near a pilgrim rest stop before they attempted to grab her and force her into the vehicle. Luckily the jogger was able to evade capture and hide in some bushes, raising the alarm shortly afterwards, but a subsequent search by police for her assailants yielded nothing. Another woman, a 60-year-old German, also reported seeing a man following her in a white car whilst masturbating but, fortunately for her, a group of Irish pilgrims up ahead was able to intervene, albeit too late to catch the man. The group was prompted to come forward with pictures they had taken of the car after they heard the news about the disappearance of Denise Thiem. Again, just a few weeks before Thiem went missing, another pilgrim commented in an online Camino forum about being lured away from the trail by a fake yellow painted arrow, after which she was attacked by a strange man with a stun gun before managing to escape. These harrowing tales of other women being approached in such a menacing way was enough for Cedric to fear the worst. Since Thiem's disappearance, pilgrims were being warned not to walk alone, particularly in the roughly 15-mile stretch in which all of these incidents took place. Despite this kind of incident being incredibly rare, the numbers walking the Camino every year are north of 10,000, so safety concerns were naturally raised, particularly for women and those travelling alone.

Thiem had quit her corporate job in November 2014 to take a round-the-world trip. At the time of her disappearance, she was on the European leg, after already visiting Singapore, Cambodia and the Philippines, during which she conversed with her brother back in Arizona almost daily. On the last day she was seen alive, the 5th of April, Easter Sunday, she had eaten breakfast with a fellow pilgrim in Astorga before celebrating mass there. Afterwards, the two went their separate ways, and she was never seen alive again. Less than a week after the discovery of her body, the Thiem family made their own pilgrimage to Santiago for a funeral mass for Denise in the magnificent cathedral that she never got to see.

It was two years to the day that justice finally caught up with Muñoz when a jury in the city of Leon found him guilty of the murder of Denise Thiem. They almost unanimously agreed that he had beaten the 41-year-old to death with a large stick before removing her hands (which were never found) and burying her body. Muñoz himself had refused to testify in his own defence but had earlier put forward a feeble explanation that Thiem had accidentally come across his home near the village of Castrillo de los Polvazares after becoming lost somewhere between Astorga and El Ganso. Muñoz further claimed to have offered to show Thiem the way back to the trail, but after she became nervous, he "hit her with a stick" — a detail that would later be corroborated by a Chinese pilgrim who had almost become a victim of Muñoz in a similar manner. Muñoz never explained why he killed Thiem but has always maintained that he did not sexually assault his victim before disposing of the body in a wooded area, possibly in the hopes wild animals would take care of the rest. In April 2017, Muñoz was sentenced to 23 years in prison for the robbery and murder of Denise Thiem.

Death is not an unknown quantity on the Camino, and at least a few of its half a million pilgrims each year are statistically bound to expire mid-walk. It was believed in the middle ages that a pilgrim who died on the Way to Santiago would bypass purgatory and ascend straight to heaven, which I hope serves as a comfort to those bereft of loved ones who merely sought to kneel at the remains of a saint.

I have a bit of a fascination with all things morbid, so while researching the murder of Denise Thiem for this book, I decided to see if anyone else had been the victim of homicide while walking the Camino. It turned out there had — sort of. In 2016, 41-year-old Jeroen Schelstraete from Gent, Belgium, was killed mid-way through his ninth Camino by an apparent hit-and-run driver before his body was found hidden under a pile of compost at a recycling plant in San Román de la Vega on the outskirts of Astorga. Police investigated his death as a murder due to the apparent attempt to hide the body, combined with the fact Jeroen was also robbed of money, papers and medication a few days prior. Tragically, Jeroen left behind a devastated fiancée whom he was to marry after this pilgrimage. Wendy Leung had walked part of this Camino with him, but he was to finish the rest without her, regularly calling and texting to inform her of his progress. She stated that Jeroen planned to get to Santiago and then on to Finisterre but was robbed of his possessions with over 250km to go. In some apparent confusion, the Gent native was arrested for harassing other pilgrims before being released later that day in a "confused state", according to the police report, possibly due to his missed medication. This was the last known sighting of the former harbour worker, with the confused state being a possible explanation of how he was struck by a car while walking late at night, perhaps in haste to make back the time he lost. In any case, police were sure that whoever collided with him that night, for whatever reason, decided to conceal his lifeless body amongst the refuse, possibly in the hopes the evidence would be destroyed by the incinerator.

Before long, this research was leading me down a 'rabbit hole' of death on the Camino, resulting in this helpful and informative countdown of the 5 things most likely to kill you while walking The Way. Please bear in mind that records of people dying mid-pilgrimage are only available on the Spanish federal website, are incomplete and only go back to 1989.

5. Nefarious/suspicious circumstances

If the list were longer, I would say that this would be the Denise Thiems of this world, but I have included the previously mentioned hit-and-run victim, Jeroen Scelstraete, along with 41-year-old South Korean Ja Ha Cho, who disappeared under suspicious circumstances from the beach at Finisterre in September 2016, and whose body was never recovered. I have included this case because, in all my research, I could find no mention of any other missing pilgrims that were not discovered eventually, dead or alive. Statistically, the chances of falling into this category are less than one in a million — roughly the same chance as tossing a coin and getting 20 tails in a row.

4. Illness

On the 11th of July 2002, Jose Maria Otero of Cádiz, Spain, died at a hostel in Rabanal, about an hours drive from Ponferrada. The apparent cause of death was meningitis. All told, eight pilgrims have perished on the trail due to some kind of illness, with only one case from being terminal, an Italian man who just about made it to Santiago before succumbing to cancer in 2004. Whether it be cancer or a bout of meningitis, sickness and disease doesn't care where you are or what you are doing. If you are worried about this happening to you, take care the next time you use a toilet — you are about as likely to be injured using it somehow as you are becoming deathly ill during your Camino.

3. During Sleep

Yes, you read that correctly. If you want to survive the Camino, try and avoid going to sleep as even the sandman is after you. About a day's walk before Santiago, at O Pedrouzo, you will find a shrine including a line from the W.B Yeats poem, The Lake Isle of Innisfree, displayed on a plaque dedicated to Myra Brennan, a 52-year-old woman from Sligo, Ireland, who died peacefully in her sleep in June 2003 the night she completed her second Camino. In total, 15 people have met their end this way, which puts it on a par with the likelihood of a mother having conjoined twins born to her.

2. Accidental Death

Santino Joseph Campo and Julian Manzano were two lifelong friends travelling part of the Portuguese route by train when it derailed on the 21st of August 2006, killing them and four other people and injuring over 200 others. Away from the rails, of the 33 people in the record books that have died as a result of an accident, 26 of them were hit by a car. It should come as no surprise that the majority of these deaths were cyclists as nearly all of their Camino comes on a road, but walkers have been known to come a cropper this way. While there are not too many instances where you are actually walking along a roadside for protracted periods, there are several examples of where the trail crosses a road, and there were a few occasions where I got into such a rhythm that I forgot myself and walked straight out into one. Notwithstanding, just because you are paying attention, it doesn't mean the driver is. When one such driver almost drifted into me as I walked along a stretch of road, I briefly considered advising, "Perhaps you should pay more attention, as you almost inadvertently occupied the same space as me on the roadside!". However, since I only had half a second, I just shouted, "Wanker!" This lapse in concentration combined with speeding drivers on rural roads makes for a dangerous mix. Heatstroke and drowning have also been included in this total despite making up a handful of accidental deaths. If you are worried about being struck by lightning at some point in your life, don't walk the Way, as the odds are about the same for both.

1. Sudden Death

63-year-old Torremocha Carlos Lorenzo died of a heart attack in Madrid on the 8th of January 2006, just 15km into his Camino, which began at his own front door. If I was to be honest, this would be the way I would shuffle off this mortal coil mid-pilgrimage if given a choice. This has happened to 35 dearly departed pilgrims, putting the odds of this happening on your Camino about as likely as being born with an extra finger or toe. However, the fact that almost all cases were suspected heart attacks, trying to undertake rigorous and sustained exercise while not in the physical condition to do so, probably increases that dramatically. Not knowing how or when death will come for you takes the pressure off at least.

20

BIRDS OF A FEATHER

||||||||||||||||||||||||||||||||||||||||||||||||||||||||||||||||||||||||||||||||||||||||||||||||||||||

IT WAS A cold start to the first half of the day as I moved deeper into Galicia, and I now could see that the comparisons to British weather in this region were well justified. With little to no cloud coverage holding in the heat from the previous day, most days in the region unfolded in chilly temperatures that would climb steadily before reaching their maximum by noon. As I mentioned previously, it was always my intention to walk the Camino during the summer months, and I was in no doubt that Spain could get more than a little warm during summer. Indeed, it is the most popular season for pilgrims, but those favouring cooler walking days can choose the spring or autumn to walk, with some brave souls even deciding to walk in winter. The preference for summer over the other seasons are evident on the face of it — flights in and out of major airports are more frequent, and an increased number of daylight hours make it much easier for pilgrims to cover long distances. Less rainfall in the summer also makes it a more comfortable and, therefore, an unquestionably more enjoyable experience, with the added bonus of being less likely to become sick from extended periods trudging through wet and cold weather. The unexpectedly cold mornings had made for more than a few less than ideal starts to the day, and walking from six in the morning to midday brought to my mind the parable of the frog being boiled alive, whereby if a frog is placed in hot water, it will immediately try to escape, but when placed in cold water that is then heated, will not. I would start off cold before removing layers of clothes at regular intervals (stopping short of outraging public decency), happily receiving no significant amount of sunburn. That isn't to say that the weather was always predictable on The Way and, on one such occasion, I stepped inside a small grocery store to get a drink out of the heat of the day. I was in the store for no more than ten minutes but stepped outside into monsoon-like rain. As a dozen or so other shoppers and I noisily jostled for the best position to avoid the downpour, I tried to ignore the silent judging of my fellow patrons for me taking up valuable space attempting to keep my enormous rucksack dry.

I was thankful that the baking heat was abating now that I was nearing the end of the Camino with its cooler Atlantic climate and could now understand the appeal of walking either side of the summer. In theory, since fewer pilgrims decide to walk during these periods, one could enjoy the feeling of being a bit more isolated in order to gather one's thoughts. Naturally, most pilgrims avoid walking in winter because it is unpleasant at best and dangerous at worst, particularly when crossing the Pyrenees in the first section of the Camino Frances due to it being almost entirely covered in snow, forcing pilgrims to take the longer but safer route around. Other mountainous sections, such as the area around Leon, can become impassable on foot for the same reason and only when one reaches the low altitude and cooler weather of Galicia will the going be a little easier. In truth, there is no 'one size fits all' approach to this. The climate of the Camino is somewhat of a misnomer, in so much as The Way does not have a weather type. Conditions vary wildly from one region to the next, meaning a successful pilgrim needs to be adaptable if nothing else.

My gilet remained firmly on for the entire day's walk as the trail undulated softly amongst the clouds for the first half of the day, followed by a sharp descent in the second, as regular markers counted down the kilometres remaining to Santiago. My next overnight stop was going to be the municipality of Triacastela, but there were plenty of options if I fancied another night up in the upper atmosphere where an interesting rumour had spread regarding local restaurateurs infiltrating albergues in the region recently posing as pilgrims in order to remove cooking utensils from the kitchens, thus driving people into their establishments. Back on Earth, shortly after the village of Linares on the Alto de San Roque, you will find an enormous bronze statue of a pilgrim with his head down in the face of the formidable wind. The statue was erected in 1993 on the former site of a hermitage belonging to the saint after which the peak is named. Since the Cathedral in Santiago was built using limestone mined in Linares, I decided to follow Picaud's advice from the Codex when he advised pilgrims to "take a stone and carry it with them to Castaneda to make lime for the building of the Apostle's church." Having no idea what limestone is supposed to look like, I picked up the first small stone I saw and shoved it into my pocket. Better late than never, I guess.

Since Triacastela loosely translates to "three castles", I was disappointed to learn that none of them were still standing due to the Viking raids in the middle of the 10th century but what it lacked in castles, it more than made up for in pilgrim numbers. With a permanent population of less than 700, I wondered how a town this size could cope with a number of daily visitors that must be approaching that figure by the morning I awoke there. I suppose this was to be expected since the next major town of Sarria is the closest point to Santiago from which one can walk and still claim a Compostela but where exactly all these pilgrims were yesterday was a mystery to me because they plainly weren't on the trail when I was. But, if that first statement was true, why would they come here? Why travel to a town infinitely more challenging to get to if the minimum distance will do? The only explanation I could come up with was that enough pilgrims must have anticipated the vast crowds in Sarria and started further back to avoid it, even though if everyone did it, nobody would. The previous night I had found a reasonably priced hotel as I, as usual, didn't have the stomach to compete with other pilgrims for an albergue bed since I was now cheek to jowl with them on the trail.

I left Triacastela to find something else I could have done without — a choice of routes to take, with both paths converging about 3 miles before Sarria at the tiny village of Aguiada. The first route through Samos promised to be less eventful, albeit with fewer opportunities to take on supplies for at least the first half of the day. The second option was shorter and could arguably boast better views; however, some tricky climbs and descents would be the price. With O Cebreiro still fresh in my mind, I opted for the flatter Samos course and, although most of the pilgrims I left Triacastela with continued with me on this route, the divergence did at least thin the herd and make the trail feel slightly less congested.

The halfway point of the day found me in the village of Samos, where I was glad to spend a couple of hours away from racing for a hostel bed amid the pilgrim army. I predicted that the lack of cheap beds for the night would be inevitable no matter how fast we went, given that busloads of pilgrims would probably already be in Sarria to snap them up. Until now, I had not borne witness to a single instance where all hotels in a town had been fully booked, so I was also confident that I would soon be resuming my struggles with 100% Egyptian cotton sheets somewhere. Besides, if they all knew how uncomfortable those albergues actually were, those folks probably wouldn't be half as keen. With a population of around 12,000, Samos is in that grey area between being a village and a town. It is home to an abbey and a monastery, the difference between which can be added to the ever-mounting lists of things I didn't know before sitting down to write this book. In case you need a refresher, an abbey is home to a religious fraternity led by an abbot, whereas a monastery is a religious home for a religious fraternity led by a monk. Or an abbot. See? Clear as mud.

Something that isn't in doubt is the religious importance of the Benedictine Monastery of San Xulián de Samos. It is the oldest inhabited monastery in Spain, and its existence as part of the Germanic post-Roman Kingdom of the Suebi that is now known as Galicia dates back to the 6th century. It was originally founded by Saint Martin of Braga after he came to Galicia to preach Christianity following his pilgrimage to the Holy Land, where he had become a monk, but after being rebuilt by Bishop of Lugo, the monastery was abandoned during the Muslim invasions of the region in the 8th century. After the locale was reconquered, the monastery was granted royal protection by Asturian King Alfonso II as a reward for providing him refuge following the assassination of his father, King Fruela I, while he was a child. As was the case with many other monasteries, the golden years of San Xulián came in the middle ages, during which the abbey enjoyed tremendous wealth and influence, controlling monasteries, churches and even towns numbering in the hundreds. The centuries since have seen the monastery undergo a complete rebuilding twice due to fire of all things, once in 1558 and again in 1951.

Located on the north bank of the River Sarria, the first thing that strikes you about the abbey is the sheer enormity of the stone walls that run alongside it, making it appear castle-like on the approach. Contained within the vast complex are two cloisters, the larger of the two being dedicated to Benito Feijoo, a Benedictine monk and former resident who pioneered Spain's Age of Enlightenment of the 17th and 18th centuries. The 17th-century cloister is one of the largest in Spain and contains a large garden at the centre of which a grand statue of the monk stands. Connected to the cloister is the church and its magnificent facade, bringing together a mix of Baroque, Gothic and Renaissance styles. The second cloister, built in the Gothic style over the ruins of the Romanesque incarnation after the fire in 1558 is smaller, older and more secluded, although it did at one time see more day-to-day activity. Between the cloisters, the library, and the church, someone with more time on their hands than I had could easily spend several days here, especially if they register for one of the guided tours given by the monks themselves. The monastery is even available for overnight stays in case you missed out on San Zoilo, but I had detoured enough. The (hopefully empty) trail was calling.

As I mentioned earlier, one only needs to walk the last 100km of the Camino to be entitled to collect a certificate of completion or Compostela. Nothing unusual in that, I suppose, with over 40% of those awarded in 2014 going to pilgrims stepping their first this far from the finish line. However, what was strange to me was to see these people kitted out with more walking gear than I was. *Surely they don't buy all this hiking garb for just a few days of walking*, I mused as I marched alongside them. I saw the empty coaches parked diagonally along the roadside before I arrived in Sarria proper, their missions complete now that their cargo of fresh-faced pilgrims had long since left them for the trail. I walked the streets to find them nowhere near as busy as I expected and now felt foolish for having done so. That was until I realised that it made perfect sense for a pilgrim arriving in Sarria to start walking immediately rather than wait until the next day. I suppose I would have considered it one last hurrah the day before, but I didn't feel that way now. There is an established, unfair temptation amongst pilgrims that have walked here all the way from Saint-Jean to look down on those who choose to start here. Although it didn't bother me in the slightest, I could, at least in part, understand why some pilgrims that had just walked here from France would be a teensy bit resentful of these Johnny-come-latelys. After slogging for almost 500 miles while contending with fluctuating physical and mental conditions to get to the same place, only for your physical reward of a Compostela to be identical, it could appear uneven. Perhaps in the future, authorities might adopt a system where the further you walk, the larger your Compostela would become. How proudly some pilgrims could parade the streets of Santiago, with giant certificates not unlike those comically enormous cheques that they give to lottery winners in hand. Perhaps it was a bit unfair, but I couldn't give a shit about the sudden overcrowding of a walking path at this point. What needs to be remembered is that each person walking has their own personal circumstances, both social and economic, to contend with before deciding to come on Camino in the first place and are deserving of the same level of respect. Jobs, families and finances are all perfectly justifiable reasons to do the minimum required for a Compostela (or less), and no Camino snobbery should be allowed to make people feel otherwise. I'm looking at you, Wayne.

Fewer pilgrims than expected isn't to suggest Sarria is quiet by any means. A busy town of over 13,000 caused just as much a jolt to the senses as major cities following extended periods in rural surroundings. Once composed, I applied my tried and trusted method of judging the quality of an albergue by spending a few seconds staring at the front door. As I was checking in, a cold shiver ran down my spine when I noticed the abundance of flyers advertising bag-carrying services spread out over the desk before me, something I am confident the young man behind it spotted due to the way his gaze oscillated wildly between my eyes and the brochures for the rest of our interaction. Following this minor episode of PTSD, I reached the sleeping quarters to find my bed to be clean and comfortable, so at least I had made a good choice there. Then again, a stopped clock is right twice a day.

I made a point to get up early to avoid the next half dozen busloads of pilgrims surely making their way to Sarria, looking forward to being down to double figures in terms of kilometres remaining which gave me the psychological boost I needed. Pilgrims are well looked after during the home stretch, and one will never find themselves without ample opportunity to take on supplies from the many villages through which they will pass. Pleasantly, I found no need for them, reaching the town of Portomarín just over five hours later.

Portomarín is rather a curiosity when one compares the old town with the new. In all the places I had visited so far (and where this was possible), a new town tended to simply be an extension of the old, usually caused by a rapid and sustained period of population growth. However, in Portomarín, the old town was literally moved to create the new one. Since Roman times, the settlement had developed from two separate villages on either side of the Minho River into a single, larger town. In the 1950s, plans were put in place to build a dam on the Minho to create a reservoir over the area where Portomarín stood, putting the town at risk of becoming a gigantic watery grave. Rather sportingly, the townsfolk were at least given enough time to relocate their most historical buildings brick-by-brick to a place higher up the mountain, such as its 12th-century temple-fortress of Saint John and Chapel of Saint Peter. Everything else was to be built again as new, but many of the less fortunate ancient features, such as the old Roman bridge, can still be seen in their original position during summer when the river level is low. In June 2013, exactly one year before my visit, 'New Portomarín' celebrated its 50th anniversary. Not wanting to take any chances in finding a bed for the night post-Sarria, I headed straight for one of Portomarín's many private albergues.

During dinner that evening, I talked with a retired Spanish couple with an encyclopaedic knowledge of the area in the middle of their 10th Camino. They told me that since the 15th century, the forested area of the Camino Frances that comes immediately after Portomarín was known as a place where prostitutes would ply their trade to passing pilgrims and how it is even mentioned in the Codex. The world's oldest profession was a serious crime in those days, and punishment for practising it would often involve those women having their noses cut off and forcing them to wear shawls over their faces to hide their disfigurement. As we parted ways after dinner, the wife told me to watch out for shawled women tomorrow in a way that was too deadpan for me to tell whether or not she was taking the piss. Doubtful that such a thing could be found in the Codex, I searched for it when I got back to my room and was surprised to learn it was true. On the topic, Picaud writes,

> Harlots who go out to meet pilgrims in wild parts between
> Portomarín and Palas de Rei for this purpose should not only be
> excommunicated, but also stripped of everything and exposed
> to public ridicule, after having their noses cut off.

The following day, I did not see any women, shawled or otherwise, in the woods after leaving Portomarín, nor the 10km of asphalted trail that followed, much of it along the side of the road. In fact, I didn't see much of interest at all during what was a mercifully easy walk. The pilgrim cemetery for those that have died along the way is probably worth a few minutes of your time, as is the detour from Portos to see the 12th century Church of El Salvador, which once belonged to the Order of Santiago — that is if you haven't had your fill of churches yet of course. Frankly, I was rather grateful for a day that was nothing to write home about and was beyond doubt that enough excitement lay in the coming week that would see the culmination of my Camino.

I was as close as I was going to get to the city of Lugo (after which the province is named) by the time I arrived in the town of Palas de Rei. The settlement has a population of between three and four thousand and was once important enough for someone to ensure its protection by building a castle. Palas even gets a mention in the Codex, where it is referred to as the beginning of the final stage of the Camino instead of the current consensus of Sarria. The town's name comes from *Pallatium Regis*, meaning Royal Palace. It was once home to the Visigoth King of Hispania, Wittiza, early in the 8th century and was an important seat of Galician nobility. Although its importance has diminished over the centuries, Palas still holds its own when it comes to remaining places of interest. The Church of Vilar de Donas was erected by the Order of Santiago in the 12th century as a monastic temple and was added to the national list of properties of cultural interest in 1931. On the banks of the Río Pambre stands the Castle of Pambre, one of the best-preserved examples of Galician military architecture in the region. Local legend tells us that the castle was built in one night in 1375 by Gonzalo Ozores of Ulloa and was one of the only fortresses to survive the Irmandiña revolts against the nobility of the 15th century and has been open to the public since 2011 following its purchase by the local government. After receiving directions from a Spanish tourist that I did not need, ask for or understand, I enjoyed my pilgrim menu at a restaurant called Mesón A Forxa after it was recommended to me by a man standing directly outside it. It was here I enjoyed sumptuous Galician cuisine of soup and roast lamb with the obligatory bottle of local wine before retiring to my private albergue for the night.

I am unsure whether the long yet undemanding days that followed were due to my body becoming accustomed to walking or if the terrain was actually becoming easier, particularly since, on many of the days, much of the heat was blocked by the abundance of oak and eucalyptus trees. Something I do know is that a few of the copious number of rest stops I was now encountering would have been nice to have had to break up the Meseta. Most of the villages or hamlets that were popping up almost as often as the stone markers counting me down to Santiago were doing so unexplored, which was a shame due to the many probable places of religious and historical significance I was missing out on. One such example is the village of San Xulián.

As the story goes, a young nobleman was out hunting when a deer in the forest foretold that the man would one day kill his own parents. The noble believed the deer's words (as would we all) and walked non-stop for fifty days to ensure his mother and father's safety, ending up in Galicia. Now, the young man neglected to let his parents in on the plan and, understandably perplexed, they eventually set off to look for him (albeit after a 20-year wait), during which time he had found work and married a wealthy young widow. When the parents arrived at their son's home to find his wife alone, they explained the situation and a big laugh was had by all. The wife was delighted to finally meet her in-laws and offered them her marital bed for the night, but when the son came home to find the couple in his bed, he mistakenly believed it to be his wife in bed with another man, killing the pair in a fit of rage. Realising his mistake, the man took his wife with him to Rome to seek forgiveness from the Pope, who ordered him to go home to care for pilgrims on the way to Santiago, work for which he was not only forgiven but eventually canonised as Saint Julian.

Just after the midway point of the day, I reached Melide, a busy market town sprawled across 26 small parishes, where the Camino

Frances joins up with that of another, the Camino Primitivo, without any perceptible increase in pilgrim traffic. Early in the 14th century, a project began with the objective of fortifying the village with the building of a castle using money raised by unpopular taxes. However, this fortress would not be as fortunate as the one in Palas de Rei, being destroyed by the Irmandiña revolts in 1467. Shortly before my overnight stopping point, I reached the town of Castañeda. It was here I would have swapped the alleged limestone I found just before Triacastela with lime that had been processed in the furnaces, carrying it on to Santiago for use in building the cathedral. Since I was nearly 900 years too late, I decided to leave my stone firmly at the bottom of my backpack and march on to Arzúa, the last major town I would enter before Santiago.

When I reached Arzúa, I walked down the main street feeling tired and hungry and was delighted to find a hotel/restaurant that could help me with both. An unsmiling curmudgeon of man checked me in while I stood before the deli counter studying the menu, from which *Patatas Bravas* jumped out at me. This was a dish I always wanted to try and, since I might not have a chance to do so again, I ordered it alongside a refreshing cerveza to nurse while I waited. As Victor Meldrew poured my drink, he scolded me for not being a mind-reader by sitting at the specific plastic chair he wanted me to, despite being the only customer in the entire restaurant. The beer he brought over looked small enough to put in a child's lunchbox, giving me enough time to drink several before the food arrived. Eventually, a dismal meal of soggy chips smothered in cheap ketchup was placed in front of me, which I ate solely because the man who served it also had the key to my bedroom.

I knew that Santiago was only a day's walk from Arzúa but was mindful that I would have less time (and even less inclination) to explore if I did not arrive there until mid-afternoon. It was for this reason that I had deliberately walked further than usual on the penultimate day of my journey in order to give myself an easier crossing of the finish line into Santiago that was free of crowds, treating myself to regular breaks. When I stopped for a coffee at a bar called Casa Verde in the town of Salceda, I met an adorable lady named Sonia who, as far as I am aware, provides pilgrims with the only hand-drawn 'stamp' available for their pilgrim passport. Hanging down from just about every square inch of ceiling space were t-shirts and flags covered with little messages and left by pilgrims before the final push to Santiago. I had coffee and left €1 for a tip even though I am never sure how to behave on the continent regarding this aspect of restaurant etiquette. To my utter surprise, upon seeing this, Sonia and her husband (I assume) did an adorable little routine where she whistled and rang a bell before jumping up to put the coin in a little bucket hanging above the bar. Not wanting to overdo it, I only left three or four more tips after that. The cafe was packed with pilgrims who soon began forming an orderly queue to have a go themselves, at which point I slinked away out of guilt. After another couple of hours walk, I found a picturesque little village called Amenal in which to lay my head before my final day as a pilgrim. On the approach to Amenal, the trail passes under N-547 road and, on the walls of the tunnel, two Scottish pilgrims had spray-painted their social media handles on the wall, inviting anyone who had encountered them along the way to upload pictures and video, although a brief check at the time revealed people were yet to do so, which was a shame. I re-emerged from the subway to find myself directly outside the Hotel Restaurant Amenal, where I was given a cosy room in an annexe building at the back of the property.

A Spanish colleague of mine had recommended not leaving this part of the country without trying the grilled prawns for which Galicia is famous. I was still yet to do so and, since it was claimed on the hotel restaurant menu that this happened to be a speciality of theirs, I made an order. What I did not anticipate was having to peel them myself (around fifty of them), and my appetite for them was gone long before I completed my rubbish attempt at doing so. Based on the look on his face that was equal parts bemused and amused, the waiter was in no doubt that I didn't have a clue what I was doing and, by the taste of them, I would certainly have to agree. The sub-plot to my disappointing meal were the antics of a local man sitting at the bar behind me, who became more and more belligerently drunk as the evening progressed. When the staff were unable to persuade him to leave after the third time the ground had risen up to meet him, the barman called for reinforcements in the form of the police and, within minutes, two officers arrived to (one would assume) 'encourage' the man to go home. To my surprise, the officers seemed to know the man and, whilst still on duty, sat down beside him, ordering their own drinks from the mystified barkeep. After the drunk man suddenly and loudly began crying, I looked over to see that he was inexplicably shoeless, now resembling a giant, bearded toddler to whom coordination and full control of his bowels were mere notions. At the time, it felt as if my cue to go to bed had arrived, although, in hindsight, I wish I had stayed around to see how that scenario played out.

I was awoken on my final morning of the Camino by the sound of heavy rain and made the short-sighted decision to wait until it died down. Not only did the downpour become worse, but hundreds of other rain poncho-clad pilgrims had also reached Amenal by now, and I was now at the centre of the swarm — the exact situation that I wanted to avoid. Dozens of people had now packed into the same small bar area that I had had to myself the night before to get out of the wet and, as I stepped out the door with only a gilet between myself and the rain, it became clear that the most significant thing separating me from everyone else was my obvious unpreparedness for the weather. I wasn't the only one not enjoying themselves, however, with the jubilant atmosphere I expected during the final push to our terminus feeling more like a funeral procession. How peculiar it was to be surrounded by people, silently trudging through the pouring rain, as if I was on my way to a woebegone music festival instead of the final resting place of a Saint. About 10km before Santiago, I passed the city's International airport, to which I would be returning in a few days to catch my flight home. The surrounding area contains the village of Lavacolla, so mentioned by Picaud in the Codex as a place where pilgrims would wash themselves in preparation to enter the cathedral. I decided that the sheets of rain falling down on me made stopping there unnecessary.

The final place of interest before reaching Santiago proper is Monte de Gozo. Meaning "Hill of Joy", it is the piece of high ground that at long last gives pilgrims their first glimpse of Santiago Cathedral, from which medieval pilgrims would have cried out with joy. Built amongst the eucalyptus trees on top of the hill is the Monte de Gozo Holiday City, a 500-bed pilgrim hostel and camping ground containing a 40,000 capacity outdoor music venue. Although the hotel has provided much-needed accommodation to pilgrims, the development has had its fair share of criticism, particularly from the church, who believe its presence to be a blight on the skyline as well as a distraction to the cathedral. From the top of the hill, I couldn't comment on its appearance but, if I had known of its existence, I would have seriously considered staying here instead of Amenal due to its close proximity to Santiago alone. A brief pause in the rain gave me a final moment to contemplate what I had achieved over the last four weeks. From here, it was only a three-kilometre walk downhill to the city centre. The end was in sight.

21

NOT ONE STEP MORE

|||||||||||||||||||||||||||||||||||||||||||||||||||||||||||||||||||||||||||||||||||||||||||||||||||||||||||||||||||||

LITERALLY MEANING "ST James of the Field of Stars", I was surprised to learn that the old city of Santiago de Compostela only achieved UNESCO World Heritage Site status as recently as 1985, one year after my birth. Santiago owes its name to St James the Great, who is generally acknowledged as the first of Christ's apostles to be martyred. Located in the temperate climate of Northwestern Spain, the capital of Galicia has been known as the finishing line of the Camino de Santiago for Catholic pilgrims since the 9th century for being the apparent final resting place for the remains of the apostle St. James. Consecrated in 1211, the remains lie within the cathedral located within the city's old town. The view down on the old city from atop the cathedral was certainly something to behold, and even amongst the heavy renovation of the cathedral, the view from all sides was magnificent. The winding medieval streets lined with tavernas and souvenir shops, busting with pilgrims, were most endearing, particularly when viewed in the rain as recommended by the locals. As it happened, it did rain plenty while I was there, and I would be inclined to agree.

Santiago de Compostela sits on the site of a 4th century Roman cemetery occupied by the Suebi, who settled in the areas known as Galicia and Portugal in the immediate years following the collapse of the Roman empire. In the 6th century, the settlement in the modern municipality of Padron came under the control of the Bishop of Iria Flavia under the orders of King Theodomar. It became part of the annexing of the whole Suebi Kingdom in 585 AD by Leovigild, the Visigothic King of Hispania and Septimania, who henceforth became the King of Galicia. In the 8th century, the region was absorbed into the Kingdom of Asturias, and it was during this time that the remains that were to be attributed to St James were discovered. It was a Benedictine monk named Usuard who first noted the settlement to be a centre for pilgrimage, not be known as Compostela until the 10th century.

In the centuries that followed, Compostela became more relevant politically and militarily, particularly after the ministerial power of the Asturian kingdom moved to Leon from Oviedo in 910 AD, where it became the site for the acclimation of several kings of Galicia and Leon. By the time of Alfonso VII in 1111, Compostela had become the capital of Galicia, and it was during this time that the town became a target for Viking raiders, prompting the eventual building of a walled fortress by Bishop Sisenand II. Despite this, Santiago was partially destroyed by the leader of the Andalusians, Almanzor, with the help of Christian lords. Surprisingly, the remains of the apostle did not appear to be a motive for the attack, and Compostela was re-fortified with defensive towers midway through the 11th century. While never to be considered on par with Jerusalem or Rome, historians generally agree that Compostela as a place of pilgrimage was in full swing by this time and when the cult of St James really gathered pace. It is from this time that the thousand-year-old pilgrimage to the shrine of St James in the cathedral of Santiago de Compostela began. Routes have since been established from all over Europe and the world, attracting over 100,000 pilgrims to the city every year.

In the 12th century, Compostela became an archdiocese, attracting a large and multinational populace. Under the new dignitary, Diego Gelmírez, the townspeople were defiant in their insistence on self-government. Near-constant fighting against the church's authority would eventually backfire for the citizens, however, culminating in the execution of the town's councillors by Berenger de Ladore in the 14th century. De Ladore would not be the only French scourge on the city, though, as the Napoleonic wars of the 19th century resulted in Compostela being sacked and captured, causing the remains of St James to be almost lost after they were hidden in the crypts of the cathedral for nearly a century.

Much of the Story of St James' burial is the stuff of legend. While no one can be certain how or why his remains ended up where they did, historians generally agree that at some point, his headless corpse was brought by ship to Galicia for burial. As recorded in the Codex Calixtinus, St James was beheaded after returning to the Holy Land from preaching in Galicia. If miracles are to be believed, a magnificent stone ship spirited his disciples (now in possession of the apostle's headless corpse) from Jaffa back to Iria Flavia in Galicia. Once they arrived, the disciple asked the local pagan queen for permission to bury the body on her land, who agreed and provided them with oxen to carry the body to the place where Santiago now stands. Almost in contradiction, the Vatican stays neutral as to whether the remains are definitely those of St James (despite Pope Leo XIII accepting them as such), yet simultaneously promotes spiritual pilgrimage to the site, with Pope Benedict XVI visiting in 2010. The cathedral itself borders the central plaza of the 'old town', and it is clear to see that this was the focal point from which Santiago and the surrounding metropolitan was developed. According to medieval legend, it wasn't until some point early in the 9th century that the remains were discovered at the site, however. It is said that a hermit by the name of Pelagius was guided to the apostle's final resting place by a star in the night's sky and, upon discovery, reported his find to the Bishop Theodemar of Iria, who confirmed the identity to be that of St James. Upon hearing the news, King Alfonso II ordered a cathedral to be built at the site of the remains, emboldening the Catholic stronghold in northern Spain in their ongoing war with the Moors and in the subsequent years, the city of Santiago to Compostela only grew.

Because my final day of walking had turned into such a slog due to the weather, my entry into Santiago had become somewhat of an anti-climax and was certainly not as grand as I had expected. No one heralded my achievement, no fanfare was forthcoming. On the roadside as you near the city centre, there is a structure made from metal grating on which large red letters spell out SANTIAGO de COMPOSTELA. With my head down to shield my face from the driving rain, I would have missed the sign entirely if I hadn't walked into the back of a pilgrim queuing up to have his picture taken in front of it.

I was particularly glad that I had anticipated the swell in the number of tourists and had my wife find and book a hotel before my arrival, as Santiago is a notoriously difficult city to find last-minute accommodation in, especially since multiple nights stays are largely not permitted in the albergues. I would be spending the first post-pilgrim night of my life at the not-at-all exotic-sounding Barbantes Libredon Hotel and, as usual, struggled to find my destination. A fitting end perhaps since I was so accustomed to feeling lost, it was becoming almost nostalgic. I did not make it to Santiago in time for the early pilgrims mass at noon and would have to settle for the later of the twice-daily services at 7:30pm. I used the extra time to shower and change before heading out to the Pilgrim's Reception Office to claim the ultimate prize for a pilgrim — the Compostela. The pilgrim passport that I had guarded with my life since it fell into the hands of a certain priest had almost disintegrated due to that day's rain but, to my relief, the assistant at the pilgrim office did not bat an eye at the damage as he asked a few questions before taking a small donation. And that was it. I had walked in as a pilgrim, and out as a tourist, only now I was in possession of my very own Compostela, and I couldn't have been more thrilled.

The text of the Compostela reads as follows:

CAPITULUM hujus Almae Apostolicae et Metropolitanae Ecclesiae Compostellanae sigilli Altaris Beati Jacobi Apostoli custos, ut omnibus Fidelibus et Perigrinis ex toto terrarum Orbe, devotionis affectu vel voti cosa, ad limina Apostoli Nostri Hispaniarum Patroni ac Tutelaris SANCTI JACOBI convenientibus, authenticas visitationis litteras expediat, omnibus et singulis praesentes inspecturis, notum facit: (Latin version of name of recipient) Hoc sacratissimum Templum pietatis causa devote visitasse.

In quorum fidem praesentes litteras, sigillo ejusdem Sanctae Ecclesiae munitas, ei confero.

Datum Compostellae die (day) mensis (month) anno Dni (year)
Canonicus Deputatus pro Peregrinis

And for those of you who didn't attend a grammar school, here is an English translation;

The Chapter of this Holy Apostolic and Metropolitan Cathedral of Compostela, custodian of the seal of the Altar of St. James, to all the Faithful and pilgrims who arrive from anywhere on the Orb of the Earth with an attitude of devotion or because of a vow or promise to make a pilgrimage to the Tomb of the Apostle, Our

Patron Saint and Protector of Spain, recognises before all who observe this document that: (Latin version of name of recipient) has devotedly visited this most sacred temple with Christian sentiment (pietatis causa).

In witness whereof I present this document endorsed with the seal of this same Holy Church.

Issued in Santiago de Compostela on (day) of (month) in the year of our Lord (year).

Deputy Canon for Pilgrims.

I had passed the time in the long queue chatting to Lisa, a nurse from Melbourne who had completed the Camino by bike that day herself. After leaving the office, we attended the later pilgrims mass together at Santiago's magnificent cathedral, which was disappointingly covered in scaffolding as part of extensive restoration works set for completion in 2020. Lisa and I soon became acquainted not only with each other but also a highlight of the pilgrim mass known as The Swinging of the Botafumeiro. During the service, a vast incense burner supported by six long ropes, each controlled by red-robed men known as Tiraboleiros, was swung above our heads along the entire length of the cathedral before rising up to the rafters back towards the altar, filling the church with sweet smoke. Apparently, I can count myself lucky at being able to witness such a custom, as it is not always the case that the ritual will take place unless sufficient donations (rumoured to be anywhere up to €400) have been raised in advance of the mass. The church was almost completely packed out by worshipers in stark contrast to the general dwindling numbers celebrating mass each week worldwide. In Europe, for instance, the number of Catholics attending mass once a week has fallen sharply from 37% in 1980 to 20% in 2012, with an even greater decline coming in North America. While it can be argued that young parishioners are not replacing the old in high enough numbers, the same can be said for men entering the vocation to become priests, which has fallen as a proportion of parishioners.

I had set aside a couple of days to explore the old town of Santiago and, until this point, had not appreciated how much more comfortable it was to walk around town sans heavy boots and a backpack. Naturally, my first stop was to see the remains of St James, where I was surprised to find only a handful of people doing the same and, to my eyes at least, it seemed as if the very focal point towards to which we were all walking was somewhat of an afterthought to the throngs of tourists coming and going. With plenty of time, I knelt at the specially built pew, unsure what to say, even in my own head. From there, I explored the cathedral in more depth, making sure to visit the stone pillar one is supposed to touch after completing a Camino but are no longer permitted to do so after centuries of wear and tear. No longer a pilgrim, I left the cathedral before asking myself the question every former pilgrim asks of themselves — what next?

I spent my first post-pilgrimage day sauntering around the old town listening attentively to the waiters standing outside the restaurants that lined the street adjacent to my hotel as they tried to persuade me that their pilgrim menu was the one most worthy of my crisp €10 note. As I moved along the street, I noticed that as I paid attention to one waiter, the next one in line would be watching, hoping for a slip-up as he unconsciously mouthed his well-rehearsed sales pitch, his eyes filling with hope as I moved in his direction. So involved did I become in this charade that I paid very little attention to what any of them actually said, in the end deciding to simply go around the block and back to the first restaurant. A disappointing fish-based *pilgrim's menu* was what awaited me, each course more forgettable than the last, which probably served me right.

Not sure what to do with myself next, I went back to the hotel, where I was surprised to meet Lisa again as she emerged from the room next door to mine. She had spent most of the day sleeping, exhausted from the previous day's bike ride and was only just now heading out to explore. Feeling bored and starved of company, I was glad when she invited me to come with her to try one of the many bars on Rua do Franco and, as we sat in the warm evening air of the plaza, we shared stories and a bottle of wine while I demolished a monstrous plate of grilled padron peppers. While I did so, Lisa explained how her highly-stressful nursing career saw her working upwards of 60 hours a week, which inevitably led to burnout, at which point she felt some time away was needed to recover. At great expense, Lisa had transported her own bike all the way from Australia to Saint-Jean and was going to the post office first thing tomorrow morning to arrange its return. She was initially planning to travel Europe by train, but a colleague had recommended cycling instead and, during her research of where to go, she learned about the Camino de Santiago. The rest of the story involves a lot of peddling.

Lisa and I discussed what our immediate plans were going to be now we had reached the end of our respective Caminos. Now, as I mentioned earlier, while Santiago Cathedral may be the destination, it is not necessarily the end. Former pilgrims have the option to continue their Camino by walking to the Atlantic Ocean at either Finisterre or Muxía. My plans for an optional bonus round that would take me to Finisterre had not changed, but I wasn't keen on the idea of walking there. Lisa had no interest in the notion, preferring to see a few more European sights before returning home, but to me, it would be crazy to have walked all this way and not to visit such a place, yet equally crazy to hike there. Including the journey back, it would have involved another 6 days of walking, whereas the same objective could be achieved with a few hours sitting on a bus. It was a no brainer. I had walked enough, and the next morning was going to take the 10:00 bus to the end of the world.

22

MY ONLY FRIEND, THE END

||||||||||||||||||||||||||||||||||||||||||||||||||||||||||||||||||||||||||||||||||||||||||||||||||||||||||||||||||||||||||||||

THE CHOICE OF whether to continue one's Camino beyond Santiago is
nothing new. In the middle ages, many pilgrims would choose to wash
off the dirt picked up from the trail in the ocean before returning home.
If in an alternate universe my Camino epilogue did involve walking to
Finisterre, the route would first take me from the cathedral through
the small towns and villages of Ponte Maceira, Santa Marina, Oliveira
and Cee over three days. By all accounts, the terrain is favourable for
the most part, and waymarkers are plentiful in addition to the yellow
arrows and meeting pilgrims coming the opposite way is no cause for
alarm since many of the pilgrims who walk from Santiago to Finisterre
also decide to walk back. Wayne's destination of Muxía is less popular
but slightly shorter, with the trail following the Finisterre route until it
splits at Hospital. If you want to have your cake and eat it, your third
and final option is to join the small number of pilgrims who choose to
walk to Muxía, then down to Finisterre (or vice versa). At around 30km,
it could theoretically be done in one long day, during which unrivalled

views of the wild Atlantic Ocean could be enjoyed.

Not riding in a vehicle for a sustained period in several weeks turned out to be more disorientating than I expected, and by the time we arrived in the small town of Finisterre, I was plenty car sick. At around noon, I still had time to explore the quaint little seaside town before starting the hour-long hike up the hill to Finisterre's famous lighthouse, towards which I was joined by a steady stream of tourists and pilgrims alike. The walk itself was easy enough, albeit along the side of the road where an occasional car would pass, necessitating a hasty retreat to the roadside ditch. However, although moderately strenuous, the walk was unenjoyable for another reason. It was dawning on me more with each step that this was the last day on which I would do any significant amount of walking at all. It had institutionalised me. I hated it, then accepted it and now needed it, and by the time I reached the top and my goal of the lighthouse, I was thoroughly depressed.

When I laid eyes on the final mile marker, which reads *0.0km*, my feeling turned from sadness to confusion since I had only known Santiago to be the supposed finish line. Doubting the Camino de Santiago would have a plot hole, another pilgrim already stood before the marker spotted my furrowed brow and knew what I was thinking. She suggested this marker was a mere confirmation that one's walking was finished unless they wanted to end up in the Atlantic ocean. Abruptly, a feeling of doubt washed over me. Although barely 100 metres from the ocean, should I have gone to Muxía to at least get my feet wet, thus confirming my Camino's completion by walking all the land there was to be walked? Once I had decided not to dwell on it, the overwhelming feeling shifted from melancholy to pride. I had done it, despite the fatigue and the farce. I crossed borders, vineyards, towns, cities, farms and villages. My hands had touched stones laid down by men who had done so a thousand years before. I had shaken hands and broken bread with people from all parts of the world, humans I would never have met had we all not decided to undertake this maddening, wonderful journey at the same exact moment. I wondered if they would share my feeling of being simultaneously remarkable and insignificant. As I stood at the one time end of the world, pilgrims would be taking their first steps on the Camino, others their last, with tired, joyful pilgrims struggling on at every stage in between. I became mindful of the humility I felt as I realised there was no longer a need to compare myself to any other pilgrim. There never was. The emotion of the occasion took me by surprise to such an extent, a moment at the cliff's edge to compose myself was necessary before attempting a particular time-honoured ritual.

For those pilgrims who have continued on to this supposed actual final stop on the Camino, it has become custom over the centuries to burn one's clothes or walking shoes upon reaching the cape. This tradition is attempted by hundreds of pilgrims every year despite self-evident health and safety dangers or ecological concerns and despite an enormous sign prohibiting it in twenty different languages. To me, warning that setting fire to your clothes may be dangerous was like warning that sleeping pills may cause drowsiness and judging by the volume of partially singed clothing that surrounded me, it seemed that this purifying ritual had been unsuccessful for all but a handful of the pilgrims that had reached Finisterre before I did. Nevertheless, I was determined to give it a go, and soon it came to pass that I had one last fiasco left up my sleeve. Despite causing the blisters that almost came to define the first week of walking, I decided not to burn my walking boots for sentimental (not to mention financial) reasons. Systematically, I went through every item of clothing on my person and couldn't go through with willfully destroying any of it. I was happy with the choices I made involving attire and therefore didn't believe any of it deserved such a fate after serving me so well. Eventually, I remembered the horrible blisters from the first week and decided if it wasn't going to be the boots, it had to be the socks, so I took the most worn-out pair I had and held them in one hand with the shell-adorned lighter I had purchased at a gift shop in Santiago in the other. After spending more time than I care to confess trying to set my highly flammable nylon socks ablaze without success, I ultimately admitted defeat like so many pilgrims before me. As an alternative, I wrote a short personal message, stuck it inside the socks and launched the bloody things into the Atlantic Ocean. Feeling at peace, I sat there for about half an hour, trying to take a mental photograph but alas, my Camino had lasted long enough, and the time had come to turn my back on the end of the world and go back home. As I headed back down the mountain, I stopped once more at the final mile marker to have my picture taken by a delightful pair of middle-aged French women as I stood beside the iron boot placed there in commemoration to the family of pellegrinos, of which I was now one. On the coach ride back to Santiago, we stopped for almost an hour outside a dismal, rain-swept funfair, with no explanation given for doing so. It was here I made the final diary entry on which this ripping yarn you are enjoying was to be based, while my thoughts and feelings were still fresh in my mind.

And that was it for me. My Camino's end was followed up with a Burger King meal and some crap Spanish TV. No epiphany was in my near future, but a renewed appreciation for a high-pressure shower followed by a clean pair of socks was. There seemed little point in hanging around, so from the bus station, I had gone straight to the only internet cafe in Santiago and booked my flight home for the very next day. Just to be safe, I took a taxi ride to the airport the next morning, during which the driver bombarded me with questions about the Camino as if he had never even heard of it. Once safely inside, I hung around the sparse terminal building, where the only human interaction I had was a firm scolding by airport security for taking photographs. Their ire drew the attention of a large group of nuns, who, upon hearing of my journey, praised me to the point where I was probably the closest I would ever get to feeling like a rock star. My prediction that at least one pilgrim would attempt to take home one of Pablito's walking sticks came true, as two young women ahead of me at check-in reacted with bewilderment for not being permitted to bring a 5 foot long stick onto an aircraft. Sadly, despite leaving it behind at least a dozen times, the walking pole that Jake had given me was still stuck in its extended position and also had to be relinquished, although I like to think of it still out there, helping pilgrims wherever it can. Strangely, the opposite came to be true for my own walking pole, which has steadfastly refused to budge from its collapsed position ever since my Camino, as if in apparent retirement. As the plane rose high above Santiago, I looked out over The Way as it stretched out of sight through the Spanish countryside I had spent the last month crossing, wishing a silent *Buen Camino* to all those pilgrims below.

When I landed in London Gatwick, I called my wife to see if she had arrived to collect me yet. My heart sank as she told me she couldn't get the day off work, and I would now have to wait the five hours it would take her to get down here. It was all a ruse however and, as I collected my bag and moved into the arrival area, there she was waiting for me, sign and all, making for an emotional moment that I was ill-prepared for. From there, it was to the car and home via a bucket of KFC somewhere on the M6.

I kept in touch with the crowd from Scotland and even visited them the following summer. My now pregnant wife and I met up with Derek at Trevor and Leanne's beautiful home in Dundee, and it was wonderful to see them all again and regale them with tales of my misadventures after our ways parted. From there, we proceeded to Aberdeen to visit Jake and Peter, the latter of whom was heading back to the Way the very next morning. We all had dinner at Peter's house, where his wife, Moira, had incorporated pretty much everything in the fridge into one meal since they would be gone for over a week. Peter's wife and daughter would start walking from O'Cebreiro in the direction of Santiago, which would take them about a week, while Peter would start in Santiago, walking the Camino Frances backwards until he met his family. Since it was 11pm and they all had to be up at 5am, we decided to leave Peter to do his packing (of which he had done precisely none), so I never found out what the plan was after that. I even wrote to Mateo, my Spanish saviour, sending him a few gifts in appreciation for him and his family taking pity on the world's worst navigator. I never heard back from him, but I like to think of him still there, rocking out to the Sex Pistols surrounded by cherries, ever-ready to take up the mantle as the patron saint of wayward pilgrims.

If an astronaut on the International Space Station listened to the song, I'm Gonna Be (500 miles) by The Proclaimers, he or she would have travelled 500 miles in space by the time the song was over. It took me just over four weeks to walk the 507.8 miles, at an average of just over 18 miles a day (not counting near-catastrophic wrong turns). This gave me an average speed (even when sleeping) of 0.71 miles per hour, which was pretty good going, but nowhere near the quickest. That honour is unofficially claimed by a lady named Jennifer Anderson, who walked the Camino Frances in a time of 9 days, 5 hours and 29 minutes on the 7th March 2011, averaging around 53 miles a day. When you consider the average person's walking speed to be approximately 4 miles per hour, it would take over 5 days to walk the Camino non-stop, making her achievement nothing short of remarkable. I had sweated buckets but became tougher, and I have since come to compare my Camino experience to that of being the father — both might drive you to the brink of madness, but you would kill anyone who tried to take it away from you. While it would be nice to say the Camino changed my life or that I 'found myself' (or some other pretentious bollocks), the truth is it didn't. I returned to the same job and carried on with my life where I left off, while my Compostela has since been replaced as my number one prized possession by a 'World's Greatest Dad' mug. The truth remains that there is no way of knowing if I would be the man I am today without the Camino. Something I do believe , however, is that if I hadn't walked, I would almost certainly be still wishing I could. They say you regret the things you didn't do in life more than the things you did and when I look at the scallop tile attached to the front door of my house every day, I have to say I am inclined to agree.

23

THE WAY FORWARD

IIIIIIIIIIIIIIIIIIIIIIIIIIIIIIIIIIIIIIIIIIIIIIIIIIIIIIIIIIIIIIIIIIIIIIIIIIIIIIIIIIIIIIIIIIIIIIIIIIIII

IT WOULD BE nice to say that a passion for long-distance walking became a habit for me, but it didn't. Cleveland, Cotswold, Glyndŵr's, North Downs, Peddars and South Downs are just a few of the UK 'Ways' I have yet to experience. I suppose the other Camino ways will always be waiting for me should I ever lose my remaining marbles but, for the time being, that 10-mile section of the Trans Pennine Trail from Warrington to Altrincham every Good Friday would remain as close to returning to the Camino as I would probably ever get. The Trans Pennine Trail is a long-distance recreational pathway that cuts across northern England to link the Irish and North Seas, gently undulating along former disused railway lines, canal towpaths and minor roads. Although the 700,000 annual visitors are mostly walkers, plenty of cyclists and even the odd horse can be seen along its 350-mile long green corridor, leaving at least a passing resemblance to the Camino. Much like the Camino, the TPT is fun, free and well supported by local rangers based at various points, ready to lead guided tours or aid any trail user that might find themselves in any trouble. For a small fee, there is even an option to join "Friends of the Trans Pennine Trail", a group dedicated to promoting the trail and its interests (which I suppose is not too dissimilar to the donativos one would meet on Camino) and, since over a quarter of the UK population lives with 20 miles of the trail, the TPT has the potential to be just as popular.

Besides stunning villages and countryside, another noteworthy parallel to the Camino is the use of certificates and stamps to ensure one's completion of the various stages that make up the TPT. Starting out at Southport and collecting stamps along your 207-mile trek east along the main route to Hornsea will earn you a certificate, as will slightly shorter variations, including Liverpool and Hull. If you can also complete the north/south trail from Leeds to Chesterfield and optional spurs to York and Kirkburton, pat yourself on the back because, at over 370 miles, you have walked all the Trans Pennine Trail there is to walk. However, if that isn't enough for you, you might consider the Liverpool to Hull route that makes up the UK section of the almost 3000 mile long E8 European long-distance path. All you need to do first is walk from Cork to Dublin and cross the Irish Sea (I assume by boat), make your way through Wales, complete the TPT, cross the North Sea, then make your way down through the Netherlands, Germany, Austria, Slovakia, Poland, Ukraine, Romania and into Bulgaria. If you reach Turkey, you've gone too far.

The idea for the TPT was first developed in Barnsley, South Yorkshire, from which the trail is administered, although day-to-day running is generally the responsibility for the 27 local authorities through which it passes. Work began on the trail in 1989 with an initial investment of £30 million and was completed in 2001 amidst the spending spree of the Millennium Commission, a public body set up in the early nineties to help communities celebrate the turn of the millennium. Between 1993 and 2006, the group was responsible for over £2 billion worth of investment in community projects, from which the TPT received a £5 million outlay to finally ensure its £60 million completion. Much of the funds used to regenerate the trail were used in the process of converting the former railway tracks into a multi-purpose path known as a 'rail trail'. Their extended, flat features, linking larger urban areas of cultural or historical importance via coastline and national parks, make them ideal for such development, and the UK can boast one of the longest networks of such trails in Europe, with over 100 currently in use. Development of rail trails began in earnest after the Beeching cuts of the 1960s, during which around 2300 train stations and 5000 miles of track around Britain were decommissioned as a solution for what to do with lines deemed either inefficient or unprofitable due to the increased use of roads and decreased rail subsidies at the time.

Physically The Way was far from transformative, with negligible changes in my muscle tone or body fat percentage, although walking in one direction under the Spanish sun for four weeks did leave me with a noticeably darker tan on one side of my body. However, a somewhat surprising change in habit concerned my altered relationship with the divine. Growing up, I was indoctrinated into the church — going to mass was something you did without question, so transforming from a lapsed catholic to a regular church-goer was probably a more surprising side-effect than it should be for someone returning from a pilgrimage. In much the same way, I doubt I am the first former pilgrim to find themselves still caught in the habit of wishing passers-by a "Buen Camino" only to be met by puzzled expressions. When I look back at the entire endeavour overall, the Camino was, quite literally, a walking contradiction. I walked in the sun, and I walked in the rain. I hated company but also craved it. Loved walking but abhorred it at the same time. I suppose right now, my feelings are that the Camino is something I would do once, but never twice. Like donating a kidney.

During another lockdown-prompted flurry of spring cleaning, I came across a copy of *A Walk in the Woods* by Bill Bryson that a friend had given me for my birthday a few years earlier. The book chronicles Bryson's journey along the non-secular Appalachian Trail in the United States with his friend Stephen Katz and was made into a movie starring Robert Redford and Nick Nolte in 2015. At 3500km, the Appalachian National Scenic Trail is a hiking trail that is over four and a half times longer than the Camino, starting at Springer Mountain in Georgia and ending at Mount Katahdin in Maine, attracting over 2 million hikers a year. Making up part of the Triple Crown of Hiking in the United States alongside the Pacific Crest and the Continental Divide trails, the Appalachian Trail (or AT) was completed in 1937 and spans 14 states during which hikers can expect to go a week or more without passing through inhabited areas as they make their way through heavy forest and mountainous terrain. And I thought the Meseta was barren. Essentially, AT hikers fall into two groups, 'thru-hikers' and 'section-hikers'. As the name suggests, section-hikers will either select particular stretches throughout the AT to enjoy in a season or take on the entire route in multiple, smaller trips spread out over several years, if not decades. The thru-hikers goal is to cover the whole distance of the AT in one season, with a handful of lunatics each year attempting to do so before turning around and walking all the way back again. After my earlier comparison with Kevin, I suppose I would be inclined to consider myself a thru-hiker at heart. However, I fancy I wouldn't fare well in an environment that is likely to be shared with a bear at any given moment.

Maybe I could get a few more brownie points with God and set out on pilgrimage again. Whether it be following Saint Paul's Christianity-spreading trek through Turkey or Mahatma Gandhi's march through India against the British salt tax, pilgrimages are waiting to be made throughout the world. However, more intriguing to me is much closer to home in the form of Ireland's holy mountain, Croagh Patrick. Known locally as 'The Reek', the mountain of Croagh Patrick overlooks Clew Bay in County Mayo and has been a site of Christian pilgrimage in the area since Saint Patrick himself is believed to have prayed for forty days in the mid-fifth century, during which time he is said to have banished snakes from Ireland. Situated just five miles from the town of Westport, the religious importance of the mountain predates this event by at least 3000 years however, with evidence of the mountain being the terminus of countless pilgrimages stretching back to the pre-Christian era, such as the discovery of a Celtic hill fort surrounding the summit that was found during an excavation of the area in 1994. At less than 800 metres tall, it is only the fourth tallest mountain in Ireland, yet attracts around 100,000 visitors a year from all corners of the globe, a third of whom do so on the last Sunday of July, coming to make the two-hour climb to the summit on a day known as 'Reek Sunday'. A pilgrim mass can still be heard at the small church at the summit for those who choose to climb, some of whom do so barefoot in a traditional act of penance. Much like the Camino, many pilgrims can be seen carrying stones either part or all of the way to the summit before laying them in piles known as cairns as a means of atonement. If climbing the mountain barefoot is not 'pilgrimy' enough for you, consider also including the 22-mile long pilgrim path leading to Croagh Patrick. Starting at Ballintubber Abbey, the trail leads one along the bygone chariot road that once ran from Rathcroghan, the ancient seat of the Kings and Queens of the Connachta dynasty, situated near the village of Tulsk in County Roscommon, to the mountain. The abbey was built in 1216, when pilgrimage to the holy land was becoming too dangerous for Christians, with a hostel (of which only ruins remain) added to provide refuge for those looking closer to home for divinity. As time passed, more and more pilgrims wanted to negotiate the same path as Saint Patrick, with the road eventually taking on the name *Tóchar Phádraig*, meaning *Saint Patrick's Causeway*. By the 16th century, however, the causeway had begun a decline that was not halted until the extensive restorations that were completed in 1987.

If that micro-Camino isn't enough for you, you might consider upgrading to the Croagh Patrick Heritage Trail. Beginning in the town of Balla, this trail leads the walker 38 miles westwards through woodland, field and boreen to the village of Murrisk at the foothills of the mountain and, like the Camino, there are churches, castles and monuments aplenty on the way. The trail was established in 2009 and forms part of the so-called 'Celtic Camino', the traditional Irish starting point for the Santiago de Compostela Camino, and is one of Ireland's routes for which Celtic Camino Compostelas can be awarded. If pilgrims can prove they walked at least 25km of the trail in Ireland, only the 75km from A Coruña to Santiago, known as the Camino Ingles, will be necessary to claim the full Compostela. Now they tell me.

In 2018, I was invited to attend the stag weekend of an old school friend in Wroclaw, Poland, of all places. As I propped up the bar while chatting with his father, somehow the topic of the Camino came up. It was one of the rare instances that I had even thought about it, let alone talked about it with someone else but, through slurred speech and waning coordination, I relayed what I could remember about the time I went for a 'massive walk', while he hung on to my every word as much as he did the bar. The rest of the weekend came and went without the topic coming up again, and we were all just about able to shake off our biblical hangovers by the time of the wedding a few weeks later. Once the newlyweds were back from their honeymoon a few months later, the groom's parents threw a lavish party for the couple with a dozen or so guests of whom I was to be one. Almost immediately after arriving, my friend's father scrambled towards me while I was in mid-conversation, a schoolboy grin plastered over his face.

"I did it." He said as if no time had passed since our conversation in Poland.

"Did wh—?" I stammered nervously as a few bewildered guests looked on.

"The Camino!" He said, cutting me off. "Got back Friday!"

From there, he spent the next hour, oblivious to the other guests as he narrated his own adventure, with every moment from buying the kit to flying home enjoying extensive coverage. I was happy to have played a part in his decision to walk, and his enthusiasm was contagious, but one look at his wife told me she was not thrilled for the topic to be brought up again so soon, and so for her sake, I changed it.

Most of my (hopefully coherent) rambling on the Camino has been focused on its past, but what about its future? Breaking records in pilgrim numbers is nothing extraordinary, and with each passing year, the number of people walking the Way goes up without any sign of abating. Come rain or shine, people are still Santiago-bound from all corners of the globe, with male and female, rich and poor, young and old still making the journey. One apparent shift is the once Spanish-led, European monopoly being broken by Americans, Chinese, Russian and Koreans — countries that have seen their pilgrim numbers more than quadruple since 2010. Almost equally as varied are the different ways to see an increase in popularity. The Portuguese way has only had waymarkers for a little over a decade but has since become the second most travelled route to Santiago, behind the Camino Frances. Pilgrims are now catered for as never before, with almost 500 places to stay along the French route alone and nearly three times as many restaurants. From food to souvenirs to accommodation, specifically catering to the pilgrim has become huge business and, whether it deserves a place on pilgrimage or not, capitalism is alive and well on the Camino, with increased commercialisation of the very thing we are trying to hold sacred becoming inevitable as the number of visitors increases. Would it be better for no one to walk? For The Way to remain 'pure', even if that were to cause its demise? Entrepreneurs might argue that plenty of people walking the Camino do so for non-religious reasons, making their financial exploitation fair game. Perhaps it's a little churlish of me to point out there are a (figurative) million other places in the world to go for a walk without merchants muscling in on the divine. Don't get me wrong, I have no problem with people claiming to be atheists, but it does strike me as odd that some of their number would want to walk in search of a saint. Most people I know would describe themselves as non-religious, but the one issue I have with atheists lies solely with the militant variety. The kind of chap whose raison d'etre is to completely dismantle another's belief system on his or her triumphant route to being declared the smartest guy in the room. Whatever your beliefs, it is, after all, a pilgrimage. Shouldn't you be a pilgrim? To be a pilgrim is to apply discipline in the shunning of the material and, in theory, the more minimalist we are, the better the pilgrim we become. On the other hand, one should be careful not to disappear up their own arse when they accuse another of being less of a pilgrim because they listened to a podcast while walking when pilgrims a thousand years ago didn't. In the style of pilgrims past, relying on the kindness of others (like our old friend Jason) would probably be more frowned upon than paying for your 'menu Pellegrino' with a Mastercard. Minimalism is seen as a radical 'new wave' against the relentless tide of consumerism — we want to leave our comfort zone, but not by too great a distance. Let's hit the dusty trail, but retain our hourly Twitter updates (#Buen Camino!). At the same time, those sanctimonious, so-called "real pilgrims" try to dictate where we should stay or what we should wear on our feet. The Camino represents a life people long for but doesn't want. They yearn for the open road but won't give up pilates on a Tuesday. The Camino happens to you, and if you get bogged down in all the crap you were supposed to get away from, it's going to pass you by, and wouldn't that be a shame?

It turns out that I am a born consumer. Love it. Can't get enough of it. Deciding one day to walk the Camino didn't cure my value-seeking through possessions. I bought postcards (to inform my new friends that I had arrived in Santiago safely), a wall tile and a lighter — all depicting the famous Camino shell. As I stood before scores of overpriced key chains, I wondered if St James would have used one for his keys and, in all honesty, it was more difficult to separate myself from this mindset than the act of physically walking 500 miles had been. And because of this, I shopped. I bought booze, nice hotel rooms and souvenirs while on this supposed journey of self-discovery. Scores of businesses in Santiago successfully exploit people just like me and between all the souvenir shops and restaurants, a massive chunk of the city's commerce relies on the pilgrim for commercial survival. Maybe they could replace these dusty old streets with a Camino walk of fame. That ought to bring in a few quid.

Generally, The Way is like anywhere else in the sense that you get what you pay for, and I found food to be the perfect example, where a €10 meal had about €10 worth of quality. Pamplona was probably the exception, possibly because the increased competition for a pilgrim's money forced restaurants to up their game and give better value. But if that was the best, Najera was the worst. Imagine an awful paella ready meal that, upon first impressions, appeared to have been eaten once already, before being sprinkled liberally with sand, and you are on your way to understanding how bad it was, although still not bad enough for me to let go of my hard-wired sensibilities and risk offending my host by telling him as such. Because of this learned behaviour, I decided to choke down just the right amount of that garbage in such instances — making absolutely sure not to finish it in case he thought I wanted more. Eating out became commonplace on the Camino for me because of the convenience. Rare were the occasions that I even had the facilities for cooking — even more rare was my desire to do so. While I observed that cooking brought lots of pilgrims together socially, doing so was never tempting to me. The ever-popular 'El menu Pelegrino' was a staple during my pilgrimage, rarely leaving me dissatisfied. Even though those three courses were nearly always salad and fruit on either side of a dish that was almost certain to include chicken, it thankfully never became dull. The pilgrim was always offered wine or water to drink during their meal, although I never witnessed anyone opt for the latter. The extra expense was worth it to avoid the inconvenience of preparing or cleaning up afterwards but eventually took its toll financially. Just one pilgrim's menu a day added up to several hundred euros all told, not including the comfortable accommodation and generous libation to which I was treating myself. Never one for eating a big breakfast, most days I simply opted for coffee first thing in the morning (if anything at all), being perfectly happy to snack as I went as sitting down to eat a meal seemed an unnecessary waste of time until the walking was out of the way. Don't get me wrong, there was plenty of choice for those who did want to partake in a morning meal, which would usually be some sort of continental breakfast, almost certainly including meat — the warmest part of which being the welcome you got as you walked in. Anyone inclined to stop for lunch would, as I observed, usually opted for a "bocadillo" (a kind of Spanish sandwich served in a baguette) because it was quick, clean and portable. Still, I rarely bothered to stop to try one as hunger never seemed to visit me during a walking session and rewarding myself with a meal after that day's hike was so much more enjoyable because of it.

My abiding memory of the Camino is the people, the places and the almost overwhelming feeling of walking in the footsteps of history. It was the volunteers, the hospilateros and donation-based accommodation, without whom the Camino as it exists today could not be. Sadly, people's tendency to take more than they give has seen the number of this type of accommodation fall to less than a tenth of the fixed payment choices. This isn't mean-spirited, it is reality, as people who have the means generally want to keep them. The reduction in the number of free services will probably be the victim of the larger overheads that result in the increased number of pilgrims. Maybe pilgrims themselves are ruining the Camino, and even tiny provincial towns and villages will need to improve their marketing and advertising presence to survive. Not that you can blame them. Modern humans have been conditioned to be consumers from a very young age, and one shouldn't expect significant change by walking for a few weeks. There will always be people who will see beauty as an opportunity to profit instead of marvel. Unsurprisingly, the commercialisation of the Camino ramps up markedly during the last few days walk to Santiago, with more places to stay, better footpath conditions and more opportunities to shop. I was going to make a joke here about Camino apps for your smartphone, but a quick search just told me they already exist. Maybe they could add some sort of loyalty scheme where one could earn nine Compostellas and get the tenth free. *El Camino, brought to you by Coca Cola. Buen Camino*™ and so on. If boosting numbers is the only aim, perhaps we should continue on while supply keeps pace with demand. The more amenities you add, the more people will consume, which in turn will bring more revenue. Accommodation will become harder to find, which will cause prices to rise, probably pricing out less well-off pilgrims. Put simply, the Camino's success could become its downfall. Tourists are a changeable sort, and The Way could be replaced in the public zeitgeist by something else quickly and easily. Religious places or those holding large crowds of people (both of which the Camino does) are prime targets for terrorist attacks, and it seems naive to assume those inclined to carry out such atrocities would overlook the potential for mayhem. That said, maybe it won't be a sudden drop. In theory, if numbers keep going up, everyone in the world so inclined to walk the Camino will have done so, after which the numbers have to drop off. Luxury hotels will go first, followed by the basic, leaving only the volunteers and the potential for the whole cycle to repeat itself. Pristine picnic areas will become lost to nature, footpaths will go unmaintained. We will be savages. Whatever us pilgrims do, the Camino will outlive us all in some form despite our fashion and fickle ways. Years from now, people both young and old will read (or watch) our journeys on The Way — some might even sit up and take notice when a distant friend or relative regales to them their journey on the relatively unknown Camino de Santiago. Of how they were rained-on and sunburned as they talked to themselves and how they tramped relentlessly towards a horizon they would never reach. They might tell of the equal kindness they received from strangers whether they slept under blankets, canvas or stars. Perhaps the people listening to these stories will be inspired to walk themselves and tell their own friends and families, encouraging them to seek out their own Compostela. I believe the Camino will capture imaginations and spark a longing to walk in our footsteps. After all, walking hasn't really changed in the last thousand years, and I see no reason why it would in the next. Kings and queens have come and gone, as have famine and pestilence. El Camino has been walked by saints and scholars, young and old, in-laws and outlaws, often for no other reason than because it is there. War has not extinguished the flame of the Way, nor regime and ideology managed to bring a halt to those who hear her call. Commercialisation seems a trifling threat in the grand scheme when you consider everything the Camino has survived. As long as The Way exists, pilgrims will walk it, wishing each other well as they go. Remember lads, life is a Camino, and you have your whole life to walk it.

Buen Camino.

ABOUT THE AUTHOR

||||||||||||||||||||||||||||||||||||||||||||||||||||||||||||||||||||||||||||||||||||||||||||||||||||||||||

GROWING UP IN Manchester, Duncan McNamara graduated from the University of Wales in Aberystwyth with non-flying colours. He found gainful employment in video editing then project management. WALK THIS WAY is his first book. When not putting one foot in front of the other, he enjoys hurling and playing the tin whistle, but is most often found watching movies with his two girls.

OIL ON WATER PRESS
True-Life Stories and Memoir

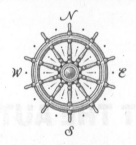

THE TOWN SLOWLY EMPTIES: On Life and Culture during Lockdown by Manash Firaq Bhattacharjee A latter-day Journal of the Plague Year. The author rekindles ties with culture, and affirms friendship, empathy and love.
pbk 978-1-909394-75-9 / 978-1-909394-76-6

SMALL TOWN SKATEPARKS by Clint Carrick A skateboarding road trip celebrating the institution of the skatepark in America's small towns.
pbk 978-1-909394-77-3 / ebk 978-1-909394-78-0

A BROOKLYN MEMOIR: My Life as a Boy by Robert Rosen Brooklyn, 1955–64: A Jewish boy learns about life and death from the W.W. II vets and Holocaust survivors who surround him.
pbk 978-1-909394-98-8 / ebk 978-1-909394-99-5

HEAVY METAL HEADBANG by Melissa Meszaros After being hit by a car on the way to a Judas Priest concert, Melissa Meszaros' life is turned upside down by a traumatic brain injury.
pbk 978-1-909394-85-8 / ebk 978-1-909394-86-5

LETTING GO THE LEASH by Stephen Ellis Hamilton Redemptive tale set against a tornado and a pandemic. Banker Stephen Ellis Hamilton quits his job of thirty-four years to save a rescue dog. And himself.
pbk 978-1-909394-87-2 / ebk 978-1-909394-88-9

A WAY UP: 1 Woman Across the Pacific NW by Paula Engborg An energetic, 41-year-old divorcee in search of Prince Charming one day finds a new sport: The Climb. Paula Engborg has barely ascended a stepladder, so why the desire to climb mountains?
pbk 978-1-909394-89-6 / ebk 978-1-909394-90-2

WALK THIS WAY by Duncan McNamara The Way is a pilgrim trail that runs 500 miles west from the French foothills of the Pyrenees to the Shrine of St James the Great. Following the death of his father, Duncan McNamara sets off with a rucksack of mostly useless items on an unusual adventure.
pbk 978-1-915316-25-7 / ebk 978-1-915316-26-4

oilonwaterpress.com

Milton Keynes UK
Ingram Content Group UK Ltd.
UKHW040000080923
428260UK00001B/60